Farm Your Front Yard

Julie McDonald

This book relates the author's experience in gardening over the last fifty years. She would be the first to declare that she is not an expert. She offers her advice for your entertainment and accrual of knowledge in battling the elements. Ultimately, each gardener makes their own decisions and learns through trial and error.

All photography by Ruth Mortenson unless otherwise noted.
Published in the United States

Published by Morten Moore Publishing
P.O. Box 881
Flagstaff, Az 86001

First Edition 2010

ISBN 0-9672576-3-8

Library of Congress # 2010942262

Contents

To my friend, Beverly Gibbs Cassady, who
in 1972 showed me the love of Jesus
through chocolate chip cookies and
changed my life forever.

Farm Your Front Yard

If gardening is genetic I certainly had a good shot at it. My grandparents were both born in Sweden in 1870. In 1887 my grandmother traveled alone to the United States, eventually settling in Galveston, Texas. After surviving the worst natural disaster in US history, the Galveston Hurricane of 1900, and helping to re-build Galveston they moved to Arizona. After work on Roosevelt Dam was completed they settled in Flagstaff purchasing a half block on the corner of Park and Santa Fe. Part of the money for that purchase came as a gift from a man who was so impressed with my grandparents' work ethic that he wanted to help them. With a small house at one end of the lot, they began to farm the back half. You can still see the beautiful old trees they planted.

My grandfather died unexpectedly on New Years Day in 1917 when my dad was two-years-old. My grandmother was left with six children, ranging in age from two to seventeen. Many people told her she would not be able to properly care for and support six children. She worked her little farm, took in laundry, did cleaning for the affluent families of Flagstaff and sewed clothing for her children after they had gone to bed. The farm provided food for the family and she sold the excess produce to local merchants. She put all six children through college on her income, selling vegetables and doing domestic work!

Growing up in this environment I learned a lot about gardening in Flagstaff. My earliest memories are of plants, flowers and trees. I don't ever remember NOT being interested in them. At age three, I remember my Aunt Julia taking me by the hand out to my grandmother's garden. She showed me a vibrant crocus, telling me, "This is the first flower of spring." I think I was born to garden!

As I grew older, we went on many family picnics in the woods but not without purpose. Everyone had a gunny sack, everyone filled their sacks with cow pies. We never came home empty handed. This was a normal family activity. I haven't been able to pass my enthusiasm for this activity on to . . . anyone. Leaves, grass and other yard waste were placed in a wheelbarrow and carried to a compost pile. Whenever possible, I caught a ride on top.

Not only did I enjoy growing things, I loved selling them. I sold my first pumpkin when I was five at the old Food-town where Beaver Street Brewery is now located. At age seven, an elderly friend asked if I would like to pick a bouquet of sweet peas, thinking I would enjoy their soft colors and pleasant fragrance. Returning home, I promptly divided them into several smaller bouquets and was out selling them to the neighbors. I got in a lot of trouble for that, although I was never really sure what I had done wrong. When I was twelve, I learned how to transplant aspens and was giving them away up and down the street.

This book is a compilation of all I have learned over fifty years of gardening in Flagstaff. I don't have a Horticultural degree. I have never taken the Master Gardening class, although I would like to do so. This is practical hands-on advice that I hope is helpful to people in Flagstaff and many other places as well! As we struggle with difficult economic times, this is the knowledge passed down from an older generation, calling to mind a time when we all moved a bit slower and enjoyed the pleasure of digging in the earth, of picking the fruit of our effort. Happy Gardening!

Chapter 1

CATCHING A VISION

During World War II, food was rationed; labor and transportation were diverted to the war effort. The effort to support our troops in Europe and the South Pacific created a shortage of fresh vegetables for many Americans. The United States government encouraged people to plant "Victory Gardens" so they could provide their own fruits and vegetables, leaving the commercially canned goods to be used for the men and women of our Armed Forces. Twenty million Americans signed up and planted gardens in front yards, in empty lots and on their roof tops. Neighbors formed cooperatives, where some would grow one thing, others something else. In 1943, nine to ten million tons of produce was grown by suburban America, equaling the commercial output raised on farms! Unfortunately, as soon as the war ended, tract homes became the status quo. The Victory Gardens died out. Boring, flat lawn replaced vibrant plots of tomatoes, squash and beans. Now, after sixty years of lying dormant, the sustainable garden is making a comeback! The front yard is not reserved for just lawn and flowers anymore!

International visitors to my home are mystified by how Americans use their property. They stand in amazement looking down my street.

"Why do people have all this grass? What do you do with it? Why don't people have gardens?"

Good question! Why don't we? In the United States, there seems to be some sort of unwritten rule stating that all the front yards should look the same, very plain with one tree, a broad stretch of lawn, shrubs under the windows with a little river rock for contrast! We see our lots as small, believing not much could be done with them. We fall into the trap of monotony, failing to think beyond our limited vision. If we have a vegetable garden it should be properly in its place in the corner of the BACK yard. Let's challenge our thinking and learn from our international friends. There are so many options. Let's build something both beautiful and edible, making the best use of a property that is far bigger and usable than we can imagine! What would YOU like to do with your property?

~ **Imagine What You Can Do With Your Property** ~
One of the best pieces of advice I have received was to grow what you want to grow! Sounds simple but often we don't do that. Let me share some of the interesting gardens I have seen where people were doing just that. For twenty-five years my in-laws lived part time in Phoenix. When visiting them, I would often walk through the neighborhood, looking at some of the more creative ideas.

In one home, the owners had converted the entire front yard into an iris garden. It was lovely! The owners often relaxed on the front porch and I would stop and chat with them about the garden. Another house had at least fifty rose bushes. Another sported a prickly cactus garden. One yard had one of every day lily imaginable.

Biologist Peter Price from the United Kingdom lives down the street. His garden is different from any yard in our neighborhood. He has packed every inch of space with plants, reserving just a tiny portion for a patch of grass. He had more in his yard than ten other houses on the street combined! My neighbor next door converted his front yard to all native plants and trees. Another home nearby has been a rental and the owner has been all too happy for me to plant the front yard.

Another friend has a vegetable garden on a busy street in front of his business. He asked that I harvest for him while he took a vacation with his family. I could barely get the harvesting done as one person after another stopped to admire lush beds and ask questions. Another home in the older section of town has a Victorian garden, complete with gates and arbors displaying the plants and flowers that were popular during that era. As in many communities, Flagstaff is seeing a resurgence of community gardens with open space being leased to those without their own lots.

So ask yourself, 'what do I like to grow? What do I want my yard to look like?' Even if your home is temporary, you can move the plants to a new home, give them away, leave mature perennials for the new owners or simply plant annuals. In the process, you are learning more of gardening and enjoying your time outside. Take a walk around your property, thinking about what you have to work with in your yard. Remember to consider porches, driveways, balconies, roofs, walls for vertical plants, steps, fences, alleys and easements. Each of these elements offers opportunity for the gardener thinking beyond a strip of grass.

Sometimes a lawn IS the best way to go. When my four children were small the yard was all lawn with a narrow strip for a flower bed. The lawn served as the neighborhood football field and I knew that was the best use of it. My toddlers spent happy hours in the sand box. The sand is now a great addition to the garden years later. As my kids got older and I had more time, I began to expand the flower beds till they were all across the front of the house. Then I began speculating about how to use the bottom of the front yard street-side, thinking about how well squash plants would do in all that sun. I decided to use just a little corner of the yard, a section of lawn caught between the sidewalk and the driveway through a process I describe in the chapter on converting lawn to garden. I started with four squash plants. I confess I was a little nervous at the time because this seemed like a radical idea. I hadn't seen it done before.

I was amazed at the response. People walked by, commenting, "Your yard is so pretty, I like your squash plants."

"I always like walking by your house, I really like those squash!"

The next year there were 10 squash plants along the sidewalk. More positive comments. When someone commented on the squash, and I wanted to say, "How about the 1,000 flowers, do you like those too?"

But I didn't. I just smiled and said, "Thank you!" Last year I had forty-five squash plants, along with beans, gourds and pumpkins in the front yard. Not a single negative comment in all that time! I notice more and more vegetables popping up in front yards throughout the neighborhood each year! One house had a lovely display of lettuce mixed in with flowers. Another expensive home had pole beans climbing up a trellis on their front porch. The vines of pumpkins ramble along green lawns. It is just a matter of time till rows of corn sprout and reach for the sky. People, for whatever reason, are feeling more comfortable being creative and expressing themselves through gardening.

One word of caution: Always start small. You can do a master plan or have a vision that may take ten years or longer. Don't try to do everything the first year. I know so many people who start out enthusiastically and try to take on too much. They find too much watering, too much weeding and harvesting. They didn't concentrate their good soil in one area but spread it out. Now their plants are somewhat feeble, producing anemic fruit. Better to start small and enjoy the effort, expanding the garden each year rather than burn out over a miserable experience with no desire ever to see a trowel again!

Chapter 2

UNDERSTANDING YOUR MICRO-CLIMATE

For some areas of the country, micro-climate is not as serious a consideration as in Flagstaff. If you live in an area where there is high humidity, little wind and relatively flat ground, micro climate has little bearing. BUT if you live in Flagstaff or a similar dry, windy, mountainous area, consideration of the micro-climate within your yard is essential in creating a successful garden.

In Flagstaff we have more varied micro-climates than some entire regions in other parts of the country! We have the "Banana Belt" at the foot of Mount Elden. The neighbor-hoods within the Banana Belt, such as Swiss Manor and Upper Greenlaw experience a 150 day growing season! Then, not ten miles from there as the crow flies, we have the "Arctic" of Flagstaff, Baderville sits in an open meadow at the base of the San Francisco Peaks with a growing season of thirty days. Neighborhoods throughout Flagstaff present a wide range between the two extremes. I refer to my own neighborhood, Cheshire, just four miles from Baderville, as the "Siberia" of Flagstaff. Cheshire is not as extreme as Baderville but still COLD. I'm afraid to find out the technical length of the growing season!

Within Cheshire there are micro-climates. I live along the Rio De Flag which is the lowest point in Cheshire. The cold air creeps off the nearby San Francisco Peaks, sinking along the creek bed, haunting back-yard gardens. My home is colder than the neighbor's home across the street. On a summer evening walk, you will feel the difference in air temperature just passing by the Rio.

In each and every home lot there are micro-climates. Depending on the direction your house faces, the exposure at different times of the year, land features, trees, fences and out buildings all come into play in considering the micro-climates within your lot. Each variety of plants has slightly different requirements. Applying what you learn about your micro-climates will enable you to match the right plant with the right location within your own yard.

First, determine the general micro-climate of your neighborhood. Knowing two things will help with this. Warm air rises and cold air sinks. If you are in a valley, you will be colder than your neighbors on a hill. I have friends whose yard is sloped and there is a huge difference between their back property line at the bottom of the hill and the top of their yard. Begin to ask questions of your neighbors, especially those that garden and have been in their homes awhile. Make use of the county home extension office.

~ Observation Is Effective ~

There is nothing like thoroughly studying your yard to get the most accurate information. Draw a map of your home. Then begin to mark the sunny, warm areas on your map. Sometimes this will be obvious as you recall where the snow melts first, where the dog sleeps on a windy day or what area dries out first.

On a day when you will be home, go out every hour and see where the direct sunlight falls and mark that on your map. It may take several days to do this. This is best done in April or May, August or September to get an overall idea of exposure. The areas receiving direct sunlight in January, may not be in direct sun during the growing season. But knowing the location of the winter sunlight is valuable in planning perennial beds.

Accurately assessing your yard is important as it is so easy to be deceived, believing an area gets lots of sun. Your potential garden site may look very sunny on your way to work and when you get home, but it was in the shade most of the day. Your prime locations are going to be where you get good morning sun that lasts until at least 1:00 or 2:00 in the afternoon. If this is next to a fence or the house, even better. The structure offers your garden some protection from the wind.

Secure your best areas for your most demanding plants, usually in the vegetable family, including tomatoes, cucumbers, basil and squash, and possibly roses. Due to living in Flagstaff's version of Siberia, I place my tomatoes next to the house. They only get sun until about noon but the wall of the house retains the warmth of the sun during the afternoon and offers protection from the wind.

The squash family will not tolerate diminished sun, demanding as much as possible to do well. They will do better when out in the open in a sunny spot which is why I place them in the front yard.

The north side may not get as much sun, but many perennials love the cool protection and moisture this exposure provides. As a rule, vegetables will not do well in the shade provided by the house so plant flowers in beds close to the structure! The southern exposure is great for lots of things, including perennials, all bulbs and perennial vegetables like asparagus and rhubarb. As the zenith of the sun is very high in the summer, the southern exposure of some homes may not get as much sun in the summer. If this is your observation, the southern exposure may be a good area for any leafy vegetables, beans, and root crops. If the back wall of the house faces the south, tomatoes may love the heat reflected during the afternoon.

The western exposure is the most difficult. It takes the hard west winds with the sun arriving mid-afternoon. I plant lots of bulbs in this area along with my most hardy perennials. I have a beautiful area under my back living room window that I really enjoy from spring to fall, but this remains the domain of all the 'tough' guys in my garden!

~ Creating Miniature Micro-Climate ~

Each area of your yard can be enhanced by the use of rocks, pots or stepping stones. In my perennial beds I use lots of stepping stones, mostly sandstone with a few flat malapais rocks. These makes it easy for me to move throughout the bed to pick flowers, weed, transplant or simply enjoy the plants. Along with providing run-off, the rock retains moisture beneath it for the neighboring plants. I've added some large rocks for interest while creating micro-climates within each patch of garden. The rock provides heat and protection on the south and east side.

The north side stays cool, moist and shady. The use of black pots, or black plastic mulch, also changes your micro-climate, increasing heat.

Start now to observe and remember that understanding the minuscule variations throughout your yard takes time. Two years ago I thought I could plant some things along the sidewalk. My perception was that this strip got a good amount of sun. I planted a twenty-foot row of beans on an area I had recently covered with cardboard, then a few inches of manure. Much to my surprise, one half of the bed lagged two weeks behind in coming up and barely produced a crop. I didn't realize that the end of the row received a lot of shade from a large white fir during the day. That area now has daffodils and columbine. Observe, experiment and remember! Then plant wisely!

Transforming the Ditch

Growing up in the Coconino Estates sub-division, I had a great time exploring the ditch that ran behind our homes. A small creek ran in the spring when there was enough snow-melt. On years with rapid snow melt, the creek sometimes flooded all of downtown Flagstaff before passing on to the Little Colorado River. It was a great place to play and have all sorts of adventures. When we moved to Cheshire in 1977, we intentionally picked a lot that bordered the ditch, near the head waters of the Rio de Flag.

The contractor who built the homes was required by law to fence the entire length of the ditch because of the safety issue. I discovered that the channel behind my house was much more active than it appeared to be a few miles south. Springs are abundant in Cheshire and the dam built by homesteaders 100 years ago keeps most of the run-off from flowing any further. A couple of years after we moved in, I persuaded my husband to put a gate in the fence. Once the gate was installed, the possibilities bloomed in front of me. When I stepped outside that gate, I might as well have been a hundred miles away in my own world. I could do whatever I wanted back there, no boundaries! After checking with the city and getting permission, I started planting trees. My neighbor, Tom

The Ditch before transformation.

Whitham, a research biologist at NAU, planted many trees for his research as well. Somehow I knew exactly what it would all look like and I led people out in the ditch, saying "Isn't it beautiful? When these trees grow up and all the bulbs are planted . . . ."

Of course all they saw were weeds, and sticks that marked the location of each baby tree! Today, thirty years later, it is just as beautiful as I knew it would be! Thousands of spring bulbs and perennial flowers are scattered along the ditch. Vegetable beds filled with the vines of winter squash, gourds and pumpkins spread along the banks. The feathery fronds of asparagus rise along with the summer squash. The wooden fence has been replaced with chain link, now covered with vines and sugar snap peas. Fifty trees provide a shady

Trees and a vibrant undergrowth create a small oasis.

arbor for both song birds and people.

I may have envisioned all this but we failed to anticipate two other beneficial results. The Audubon Society did a bird count in Flagstaff a few years ago and I understand that the largest variety of species were found in the little eco-system behind our house!

The trees and shrubs also changed the micro-climate and growing conditions along the ditch. The channel, being the lowest point in Cheshire, has some brutal frosts. The trees act as a protective cover and windbreak which has extended the growing season by several weeks. Cold air flows along the channel just like a river. When the stream of cold air hits the trees in the ditch it is stopped! The trees create a more humid environment, helping other vegetation to grow better. On a hot summer day, the ditch is usually teaming with grasshoppers and uncomfortably warm. When you walk under the cool shade of the first cottonwood, the air becomes cooler and more humid. The grasshoppers are simply gone. Grasshoppers don't like the cool shade or humidity.

There is a trail that runs along the ditch behind the houses. Many people walk or ride their bikes along the trail. I still love going out there but now there are almost as many people walking in the back as there are in the street out front. One other thing has changed. I used to drag unwilling people out to look at my dreams. Now people are asking me for a "tour of the ditch!"

Chapter 4

CONVERTING LAWN TO GARDEN

Whatever you paid for this book, this short chapter alone is worth the price! This single tip, and for the life of me I can't remember where I got it, has saved hundreds of hours of time and a boatload of frustration. NEVER try to remove grass by digging up the sod with a shovel or a roto-tiller. Manual removal is next to impossible because any roots left behind will soon sprout above the surface and spread once again. Grass, by its very nature, provides multiple nutrients to the soil. The green blades, brown thatch and thick roots are filled with nutrients which you really want to save in the soil.

Decide on an area where you would like to see a garden instead of lawn. This method applies to clover, weeds, or ground-covers and can be done any time of the year. Take cardboard boxes and break them down. Lay the cardboard flat

NEVER try to remove grass by digging with a shovel,a roto-tiller or other methods.

on the ground, overlapping the edges when using multiple sheets. One layer is sufficient but two is better. Use several layers of newspaper over gaps in the cardboard or to round square edges. MAKE SURE NO GRASS IS LEFT EX- POSED, CHECKING CAREFULLY ALONG THE EDGES OF A SIDEWALK, PATH OR DRIVEWAY. You may need to place a few rocks on top to hold the cardboard in place until you've covered this with dirt. Far easier to do this on a still day without fighting the wind.

With the cardboard and paper in place, begin piling organic material onto the cardboard. In the fall, leaves are good. A truckload of aged manure is excellent. You can use compost or garden dirt from another part of your yard. The organic material, manure and soil should be at least three inches deep. This year I had lots of partially decomposed leaves which I added to the mix.

Using a rake, smooth the compost out so that it is level and all the cardboard is covered. Add an inch of fine soil on top and then plant directly into the mixture. The layer of dirt will help the seeds germinate. In planting the bed, there are many options you can try as long as you don't break through the cardboard.

One of my favorites was a wild flower mix scattered over the manure and sprinkled gently a couple of times a day until the seeds came up. Wild flowers don't need deep soil so they thrived and were a stunning display!

Like the wild flowers, I tried a mix of cosmos scattered over the manure. Beautiful! If you're more interested in vegetables, place three or four small mounds of soil on top of the three inches of manure and plant pumpkins or gourds. They require the deeper soil provided by the mounds while the remainder of the bed stays at the three inch level. The vines get huge and cover the entire area in no time. I've found beans and lettuce have also done well.

The cardboard and deterioration of grass takes a full year to complete before you can dig in the top layers. It is important to leave the cardboard intact. Do not dig into the layers as you wait for full decomposition. After a year you may turn everything over with a garden spade. The cardboard should be completely decomposed. Remove any packing tape and discard. The grass will be dead, decomposed into the soil, leaving all of the nutrients. At that time you may use the bed for anything you want - bulbs, perennials or garden space.

Over a five-year span I converted half of my lawn into a garden and it was nearly effortless! The biggest challenge was finding sufficient organic material to cover the cardboard. As I noted, this method takes much of the more strenuous labor out of converting your lawn into a functional garden.

Chapter 3

COMPOSTING

Decomposition is a natural occurrence as life forms break down and return to organic material. I once had someone rush up to me, with a note of distress, saying, "I think I did something wrong with my compost." Compost will happen, all we are doing with a compost bin is speeding up the process.

~ Why Is Compost So Important? ~
Compost is vital in Flagstaff and other parts of the southwest because we don't have soil here, just various forms of rock and clay. The rock comes as Malapais, sandstone, limestone and cinders - none of them favorable for growing plants. Compost is much more than amending the soil, it is almost creating the soil. Like the saying, "you are what you eat", the same is true for plants. They need a loose, healthy soil for roots to grow easily and provide needed nutrition.

There are generally two problems that plague compost. The mix is either too dry or too wet. The compost pile needs to be moist, not saturated. If it is too dry, try soaking some of your ingredients in water and mixing them in the pile. If the compost is soggy, trying mixing shredded newspapers into the pile.

There are two different ways to compost and I recommend practing both forms.

~ Active Composting ~
When speaking of compost, most people refer to a bin of some sort for yard waste and kitchen scraps. Keep in mind that compost needs three square feet to internally heat the pile, maximizing decomposition. However, you can use something smaller. To make a quick, easy bin, cut off the bottom of an old plastic garbage can and turn the can

upside down with the largest circumference on the ground. I cover the top with an old air mattress, preferably a dark color to draw heat, but any non-permeable material will do. Covering the can allows us to control the amount of moisture in the compost. Compost that is too dry tends to be a problem in the arid southwest so we add water as needed.

Using a container, like a garbage can, keeps the household waste confined and the animals out. We'll call this your main compost bin. Do not add meat or dairy to the compost bin. Adding a piece of freezer-burned fish calls to memory the native Americans who taught the Pilgrims how to plant in the rocky soil of New England - better to add your fish directly to the garden.

When you wish to aerate your compost, tip the container over. Then use a garden fork to turn the compost. A shovel will work though it may compact the pile. The more frequently you turn the compost, the faster it will decompose. Turning adds oxygen while mixing the dry and moist ingredients. You can let it go for months though without disruption. I don't turn the compost at all during the summer, I am too busy in the garden. As I've planted close to the bins, I don't want to risk tipping over the bin and crushing the plants.

In June I usually plant seeds in the top of the bin. Beans are perfect for this. They grow wonderfully in the compost, producing lots of beans and adding nitrogen to the soil. Their roots, in turn, help to break down the compost. The bean plants are a reminder to add water as it would be easy to let the compost dry out. At the end of the summer the level of compost within the bin has shrunk down about a foot and is perfect, ready for next season. I lift the bin off the finished compost and may move the container to another part of the garden. Whether I move the compost or the bin, I am starting with an empty bin again.

~ Passive Composting ~
If you have access to large amounts of yard waste, a second pile for passive compost is a good idea. This means an area where you pile leaves, garden debris and weeds for months at a time. A couple of years ago I was walking

behind my house along the ditch where I have a large garden bed. I noticed a zucchini plant doing very poorly despite great exposure and plenty of water. As I examined the plant, I realized that the soil in that bed had not been amended for about ten years. That fall I began piling all the weeds I pulled in a pile where that zucchini had been. Over the next spring and summer, I added more weeds. Last year, I planted directly on the pile and had the most beautiful, healthy zucchini imaginable! A loose pile of weeds and leaves sounds unsightly but actually blends into the garden's appearance. The pile is constantly decomposing underneath the top layer so never gets very high.

If the weeds have begun to bear seed pods, most of the seeds are deep in the pile. If they germinate, they will die out for lack of sunshine. Any seeds close to the surface that might sprout are confined in a small area and can quickly be removed.

One of my favorite ingredients are bags of leaves that have been set out for bulky trash. Too much of a good thing can pose a problem. Last year, I found that the one hundred bags of leaves had not all decomposed well over the winter. I came upon a solution in mixing Starbucks*

coffee grounds with the leaves. I have a huge compost pile, using this combination, tucked into one corner of the yard. The pile is so hot this year that with our record-breaking snowfall of fifty-four inches, the snow melted into the pile in three days!

In starting your passive compost, mix the coffee grounds with the leaves. Don't leave them in a clump. (T&E)* Adding moist garden dirt and manure into the leaves helps contribute the necessary organisms to get the compost going.

Avid gardeners come to love compost and soon find they cannot generate enough to supply all their garden needs. An excellent option is to obtain manure from a stable or any grain/grass-fed animal. Avoid manures where a lot of sawdust has been used. (T&E) Sawdust breaks down very slowing, robbing the soil of nitrogen in the process. Manure mixed with straw is a good combination. If a stable is not an option, purchase the CHEAPEST steer manure from a local retailer.

It is impossible to have too much manure.

*Starbucks has a bucket set out that says "Grounds for your garden". Help yourself! If you don't see the bucket, feel free to ask if they do have grounds. Be sensitive, allowing paying customers to go ahead of you. Also, be sure to ask for the espresso pods. The grounds are in the foil bag the coffee came in but often leak. Keep a container in your car to put the grounds in. (T&E)

* T&E stands for "Trial and Error". These are things I have learned the hard way. Without going into all the gruesome, embarrassing or boring details, take my word for it.

~ Worm Composting ~

Last year at my Farm Stand, one of my customers brought me a bag of Red Wigglers. I have been amazed at what

they are doing. I wasn't quite sure what to do with them so I went on the internet and found some helpful tips. This variety of worms freezes easily so they need to be kept indoors. They are currently residing in soil in two coolers that were left out by a neighbor for Bulky Trash pick-up. I have really appreciated their efforts with all the snow as I can't even see my compost bins, much

less get to them. I've been putting food waste in the worm coolers. (Not to be confused with wine coolers.)

I didn't have enough compost to start some seedlings in January but was surprised at how much rich, dark compost the worms had already produced from the food scraps I had given them. The worm castings are rich in nutrients and create a great growing medium for any size of plant. They don't smell at all and one friend keeps them on her dryer.

I used my first batch of worm casting on a new lettuce bed. Each casting is one to two inches long and feels very spongy. In two bins growing side by side, one with worm castings, the other without, I planted lettuce this spring. The lettuce in the bin with the worm castings in early July was three inches high with each leaf perfect while the lettuce without castings only stood an inch and a half. Although I don't know that much yet about composting with the red wigglers, I am IMPRESSED!

~ Compost Ingredients ~

Kitchen Waste:
Vegetable scraps, raw or cooked
Fruit
Coffee Grounds
Tea, tea bags
Expresso
Breads, Pasta
Cereals, including cereal 'tailings'
Grains
Rice
Left-over casserole (no meat)
Left-over soup & salad
Egg Shells
Shrimp shells

Beverages:
Fruit Juice
Gatorado
Coffee, Tea
Soda Pop
Alcohol

Sweets & Treats:
Flour/sugar
Cake
Cookies
Pastry
Candy

Yard Waste:
Vegetable clippings
 flower clippings
Grass clippings
Leaves
Weeds
Plants
Garden dirt, sprinkled

Paper Products:
Newpaper
Shredded paper
Paper towels
Cardboard

Limit:
Dairy
Citrus
Onions
Sawdust
Pine Needles

Manure:
Grain-fed animals
        & their bedding
(horse, cow, goat, sheep)
Rabbit
Elk
Chickens / other birds

NO - NO - NO!
Meat
Fat
Cat & dog waste
Rose Stems

Nutrient Composition of Common Organic Materials

	Nitrogen	Phosphorus	Potassim
Blood Meal	15.0	1.3	.07
Bone Meal	4.0	21.0	.02
Cattle Manure, fresh	.3	.02	.04
Cattle Manure, dried	2.0	1.18	2.2
Coffee Grounds, dried	2.0	.4	.7
Fish Emulsion	5.0	2.0	2.0
Fish Meal	10.0	6.0	2.0
Horse Manure, fresh	.4	.2	.4
Horse Manure, composted	.7	.3	.6
Poultry Manure, dried	4.0	3.0	3.0
Rabbit Manure, dried	2.4	.06	.05
Seaweed	1.7	.08	5.0
Sewage Sludge	6.0	4.0	.0
Wood Ashes	0.0	1.5	7.0
Ammonium Nitrate	33.0	0.0	0.0
Ammonium Sulfate	21.0	0.0	0.0
Urea	45.0	0.0	0.0
Sulfur Coated Urea	32.0	0.0	0.0
Monoammonium Phosphate	11.0	48.0	0.0
Diammonium Phospate	20.0	50.0	0.0
Super Phosphate	0.0	20.0	0.0
Treble Superphosphate	0.0	45.0	0.0
Sulfate of Potash	0.0	0.0	50.0
Potassium Nitrate	13.0	0.0	44.0

Source: The Arboretum at Flagstaff #90-0

A Note on ph

You may have seen this designation which indicates whether your soil is alkaline, acidic or neutral. Vegetables and most flowers do well when soil ph is between 6 and 7.5 on a scale of 1-14. You can purchase a small kit to test your soil at any garden center. Adding gypsum or lime will help lower your ph while sulfur helps raise your ph. Generally our dry, western soils tend to be alkaline. The summer rains help neutralize the ph in our soil allowing the plants to absorb the minerals contained in the soil.

Chapter 5

PREPARING THE SOIL
AND `PLANTING YOUR GARDEN

Get ready, get set, GO! The garden really begins in December. My favorite day is in late December, usually it is snowing and blowing when I open my mailbox and there it is: my first seed catalog! Oh what a delight to see those bright, colorful pictures of beautiful flowers and wonderful vegetables. Outside the earth is white or brown, everything looks dead. Inside, I turn the pages of my garden catalog and dream of the season to come.

The time to order is: as soon as you can! There are many advantages to ordering early. With our short growing season, some veggies and flowers need to be started in January. You get a jump on supply because seed catalogs often run out of certain varieties. The ordering process gets you thinking about and planning your garden.

Compare the same items in different catalogs, there can be a big difference. Order the larger quantities and you will be amazed at the price savings. I try to buy enough to last five to seven years. This is the time to get your order in for seed potatoes and onion sets, rhubarb or asparagus plants. They may send them at a later date, but you will prepare the ground before the live stock arrives.

Sharing an order with a few garden friends is fun, allowing you to order larger quantities and save money. The bigger the order, the more you save and sharing helps reduce the shipping costs. Learn to read between the lines of the garden catalog. "Vigorous" means it is going to take over! "Compact" means that it has been hybridized to accommodate a small garden and probably won't produce much. If you have questions, call the customer service, using their toll free number. They can be very helpful in answering your questions.

~ Preparing The Soil ~

Soil preparation really goes on all year. As you move forward with composting, you will have several bins, each at a different stage of decomposition. If you are converting lawn to garden, that will be in progress as well. Yet, the most work occurs in the spring. If possible get out early in spring and turn your soil. This can be done as early as February or March, if the soil is not too saturated. The soil should be moist as it is difficult to turn dry, compacted soil. If there has not been adequate moisture you may have to wet it down. You can soak the ground and wait a couple of days to turn it.

Turning the soil benefits the garden in several ways. First, turning the soil exposes eggs or larvae of insects to frost thereby killing them. The thought of gaining a jump on grasshopper destruction is worth getting out there!

You also get a jump on weeds that have made an early appearance. Every once in a while you will find a plant that has volunteered in the garden area that you will want to transplant.

Turning the dirt aerates or add oxygen to the soil while giving us some great exercise. Since turning the soil is hard work, it is not unpleasant to do this chore on a chilly day. Doing a quick turn in the spring makes it much easier when you turn the soil again before planting. You can add compost or manure during the first turn or wait till planting. Keep a bucket for rocks that come to the surface.

As the weather turns warm and you anticipate planting seeds and seedlings, rake your garden beds fairly flat. Some vegetables prefer to be planted on a small mound so begin shaping these in preparation for planting. You will be planting in mid-March or the first week of April, and that comes surprisingly fast.

I always plant more closely than the seed packages recommend. The emerging plants seem to do just fine and this greatly increases the yield. I'm not sure who that is written for but surely someone who has a lot more land to work with than I do! I also have given up planting in rows. As I looked at my lettuce one year, I thought, "I'm doing this the wrong way. Look at all this wasted space, why don't I just scatter the seeds around in this whole area and use every bit of space?" This has worked great, and if the area is big enough I place a few stepping stones so I can get around easily to water, weed and harvest. I would recommend this with lettuce, chard, spinach, beets, carrots, beans, kale, almost all herbs, annual flowers like cosmos, zinnias and marigolds. I find it almost impossible to toss out a seedling that has been thinned so I end up moving them somewhere else.

As long as the root is intact they usually do great! Be sure to trim back their leaves so they don't have all that green to support as the root system is established. Once when I was harvesting a garden for a friend I found that someone else had come earlier in the day and thinned the chard. It was laying helpless in a heap. I took the chard home, trimmed the outer leaves and ate them. I soaked the plants over night, then planted about 60 chard in every nook and cranny I could find in my yard. Every single plant survived, grew, produced and came up the next spring.

When actually planting the seed remember that the bigger the seed, the deeper it goes. This is a helpful rule of thumb. Because of our dry climate, it is better to err on the side of planting a bit too deep than too shallow. Seed that drys out will not sprout. Also, the smaller the seed the more shallow it is planted the more you need to sprinkle it till it germinates. Larger seeds can get one good watering every few days and be fine.

~ Planting The Seed ~

Remember to soak a good number of seeds, including peas, the squash family and chard to help ensure germination. You will not see this on the seed packet or read about it in most garden magazines. Most gardeners across the US are fighting fungus and rot. They wouldn't dream of soaking seeds! Soaking the seeds makes a huge difference in our dry climate. The arid soil can cause seeds to dry out, never getting moist enough to germinate.

Lay out your garden in the way you like it, considering what works best for you and what is best for the plants. I find I use fewer rows. I am doing more "sprinkling" of seeds, then covering with a layer of fine soil. This seems to be the best use of limited space.

Place peas along a fence where they can climb the links. I plant my lettuce next to the peas. They are both spring crops so it makes it easy to water them at the same time.

Squash are scattered throughout the garden where they will thrive in the sunny, rich soil. I often place them in groups or along curving trails. Pole beans are planted where they can climb while bush beans sprout from large pots. These pots are usually filled to the top with the compost and partially decomposed leaves. After adding a two inch layer of soil on top, the bean seeds are planted very close together. This is an ideal way to raise beans. They stay clean, are easy to pick and the leaves in the compost are completely decomposed by the end of the summer. These pots are located strategically, acting as a "hose guard" to keep me from running over plants as I pull the hose through the garden.

Soak the soil thoroughly after planting the garden. The larger the seed, the less it needs water after planting. For example, after giving beans or soaked peas a good watering, you can wait several days to water again. Waiting may actually help them to germinate as wet soil stays cool. You want the soil to warm up for good germination. Tiny seeds like lettuce and some flowers are planted very shallow. These dry out quickly and need to be sprinkled once a day if possible.

Soak the soil thoroughly after planting the garden.

~ Planting In containers ~

Almost everything you can grow in the garden, you can grow in a container. That is good news if you have a small area! As discussed in the chapter on vegetables, all my tomatoes are grown in black pots. I also have two small metal water troughs with holes for drainage. I use these for lettuce, but they would be great for herbs, flowers or beans. Squash, beans, lettuce, chard, peas, herbs, flowers of all kinds can be grown in containers, some even do better in a container! In choosing the size of the container, remember how large the plant will be when it matures and the amount of space the roots will require.

Perennials should not be left over the winter in a pot outside. It is very hard on them over the winter as the pot continually gets warm then very cold. It is also difficult to keep the plant watered.

Remember three important things about container growing. Make sure the pot is adequate for what you are potting. For vegetables I like to use a pot at least 12 inches deep. for a growing medium, combine a really good soil, potting mix and compost. You will probably need to use some sort of fertilizer to provide adequate nutrition in the confined pot.

You must water every day! This is essential. A pot drys out so quickly, much faster than plants that are in the ground. Watering everything in pots needs to be part of your daily schedule.

So we've talked about preparing the soil. In the spring, you've worked in the manure and other compost elements. You may have even tenderly tucked the seeds and seedlings into the soil. Now, consider . . . .

~ Being Prepared Is Everything
In a Mountain Garden ~

The calender says today is May 21st. As I write this, we are preparing for a major cold front to pass through Flagstaff. Temperatures are predicted to drop to freezing. As this is almost an annual event in the southwest, it is good to know how to deal with "cold snaps" so that you don't loose everything you have worked for in the last few weeks.

These events are not usually confined to one cold night. They begin with wind, sometimes lasting for several days. The front may bring precipitation in the form of rain, hail, snow and sleet. This is followed by cold air with at least one or two nights of below freezing temperatures. We were all sure spring had arrived but the temperature outside feels more like winter.

This is pure misery for plants. In my experience, the cold weather crops such as lettuce, chard, peas and root crops will be fine throughout the cold snap. They might appreciate a layer of hay to protect them, if it doesn't blow away. some kind of shelter, such as a lawn chair or chaise lounge placed carefully over the lettuce will protect it from damage. A rock placed on the lawn chairs will help anchor them, preventing the winds from whisking the chairs across the garden.

Bring any tender annual or vegetables growing in pots into the garage or house. As to your garden plots, your most sensitive plants are the squash family, peppers, melons and cukes, beans and tomatoes. The key, T&E, is to cover the tender seedlings in the beginning and leave them covered for the duration. For years, I spent many hours covering my garden at night then uncovering during the day, covering again the next night, uncovering during the day . . . .Why? The plants will be blasted by wind, hailed on, frozen back for the season! This may last for a week! You'll discover in leaving the cover in place that the plants will be fine, and you will save yourself a TON of work!

Squash: In 2010, we suffered through three weeks of cold tempera-tures. Each day seemed as if summer would never arrive. I had my garden ready to go with many of the squash plants already in the ground, expecting the season to progress as normal. Earlier, I had recovered several large clear plastic containers

from the trash. I placed these over my squash with a bowl or gallon milk container filled with water alongside each plant. I did not remove containers throughout the entire three weeks.

What a reward! The growth of the plants over the next month exploded unlike anything I had ever experienced previously. Each plant was loving it's own little greenhouse. I had squash on each plant by early July. I plan to use this method next year, regardless of the duration of cold temperatures.

Remember you want to protect the "guts" of the plant, don't worry about outer leaves. If you don't have the large clear plastic containers, place some hay, dry leaves, newspaper, shredded paper or cloth to protect the inner circle of the plant. Next place a laundry basket over the plant. With really cold weather, add a light sheet on top of the basket. Again, a nice size rock will keep the basket from flying down the street with a heavy gust of wind. More rocks or watering cans will hold down the edges of the sheets. You can cover several plants with one sheet. Do this before the wind is blowing fifty miles an hour - much easier! This arrangement will protect down to about twenty degrees. If one night is especially cold, add a light blanket on top of the sheet.

When transplanting mature plants, mix compost with a little bonemeal and manure. Add a scoop of the mixture into the hole for the seedling.

If your area is expecting only a light frost, or even the potential of frost, there is nothing better than a laundry basket. T&E. It protects while letting air circulate. Avoid anything that touches the leaves directly.

Tomatoes: You know that tomatoes are very tender so be well prepared with sheet every night until temperatures stabilize in the lower 40's. Place hay or newspaper around the stem. Using clothes pins, 'swaddle' all the plants by securing the sheet to the cage wires. Make sure you have the ends covered. You may need to use a rock or lean something up against the sheet as in a heavy wind the sheet can be caught and torn or literally blown off. Use another sheet on top if it is going to be extra cold.

Using these precautions, your plants will be fine for the

duration if you leave them covered. Generally, you don't need to water them. Watering tends to make the air colder (hypothermia) and increase the chances of freezing. However, if the earth dries out, watering may become necessary.

As I mention in the section on beans, they are so difficult to cover, and have such a short growing season I like to plant in mid June, avoiding the "cold snaps". Germination is seven to ten days.

Pole beans do need to go in earlier, mid-May, but the pole can be helpful in providing a "prop" to protect them. Hay, with a sheet tied and draped from the pole usually is adequate protection.

Other ideas for protection, when you get really desperate!
- cardboad boxes secured with a rock
- ladder, with a sheet over it
- card table
- board supported on two- five gallon buckets, covered with a sheet and secured with a rock. This could protect up to 10 feet or more.
- Any lawn furniture or tables

~ Water Conservation ~

Water conservation is a huge issue to all of the inter-mountain west. Using water wisely may not have been a problem for you in the past, it could be in the future. Wise water use is important for everyone to learn in conserving a natural resource. Knowing the water requirements for different plants will help you in determining your water schedule and use. Dry years or drought can cause water shortages and rationing. You may have a family emergency which calls you away from home for several weeks. Knowing which plants to help first will be invaluable. This is water triage 101.

When considering what is most critical to water, the first priority goes to anything growing in a pot. They dry out quickly and can't go for more than a few days without water. The next priority would be annuals, including both flowers and vegetables. They become even needier if they are blooming or producing fruit.

Perennials are extremely hardy and a good, deep watering will last for weeks. They may be stressed but they will survive, especially if they are more than one year old. Here is a great tip on grass. Grass that is well-established will simply go dormant if it does not receive water. You can let it go. As soon as the rains come, or you get around to watering, the grass ends its dormant state. Neglect your lawn too often though and you may begin to lose the lush lawn some gardeners value.

Here are some more tips for using water wisely:
~ Infrequent deep watering for established plants is much better than a frequent sprinkle.

~ Put gutters around you home and collect rainwater. You don't have to have a fancy rain barrel, you can use a garbage can to collect the run-off. A screen over the top or lid when not in use keeps mosquitos or other insects and birds out. I am always rescuing lady bugs that have fallen in!

~ Plant water-loving plants near the water barrels. I have rhubarb plants near three of mine. They get loads of water that way!

~ The more water you use the more you pay per gallon, so all conservation measures pay off.

~You will often read in garden literature not to water in the evening because of mold, fungus etc. This is directed at the more humid states, and does not apply an arid climate. I would say water in the evening, especially in the hot dry months. This allows the plant to soak in the water all night long. You greatly minimize water that would be lost in our dry, windy and sunny days.

~ Black plastic not only warms the roots of many vegetables but retains moisture in the soil.

~ Develop good habits of not wasting water in the house. Quick showers, correct loads in the washing machine, full dishwasher all help to use water efficiently.

~ I always take my dishwater out to my flower bed. Plants appreciate the phosphate in dish soap!

~ Think WATER when you shovel the snow. I intentionally shovel some areas to give plants extra moisture in the spring.

~ Rocks and stepping stones increase water to all the plants around them.

~ Mulch and bark help to retain water. However, wait to add the mulch till your plants are firmly established. Adding mulch to garden beds before the seedlings are established may cool off the soil and keep them from making an appearance. Mulch will also help control the weeds and save some labor.

~ Manure and compost help to retain water in the soil.

~ I have to sleep with a hot water bottle, even in summer. The water never goes down the drain, it waters the geraniums on the front porch in summer, or in winter on the window sill. Think of ways in your own home where you could conserve water.

~ Last but not least, California's water saving slogan, "If it's yellow let it mellow, if it's brown flush it down."

DISCLAIMER
No matter how water conscious you are, every gardener needs the luxury of a nice HOT bath after a hard day of work in the garden!

Chapter 6

BEST PERENNIALS
for the MOUNTAINS OF THE SOUTHWEST

The terms perennial and annual cause more confusion among new growers. Here is an easy way to remember: Annuals are planted every year. Perennials make our yards their home. When planning a garden bed, it is not a matter of choosing one or the other. We use both in the garden to create a lovely display.

A perennial is like a friend who returns every year, bigger and better than the year before. Perennials are wonderful in so many ways! They grow in areas of the yard where annuals would struggle. They require very little care and are easier than a lawn! Although they appreciate good soil, many will tolerate a poorer soil unlike a vegetable or annual. If you plan correctly, you can have perennials in bloom from March till October! Here are some of my favorites.

Artemesia & Dusty Miller The silver green foliage of artemesia and dusty miller are a nice contrast to your other perennials. Dusty miller, on the right, tends to have a broader leaf while artemesia, below, is feathery and soft.

Both plants flower but the tiny blooms are so small that they remain unnoted next to the bolder perennials and annuals. Both prefer to be in full sun. Dusty miller may return the next year with winter protection in some of the cooler areas. Artemesia will return each year, growing in size. When it threatens to overwhelm neighbor-

ing plants, you may have to thin it.

Asiatic Lilies are the momentary stars of the garden. They shoot up with narrow leaves sprouting individually from a stem that may reach four feet high with sufficient nutrients in the soil. Their blooms are spectacular in combinations of yellow, white, pink and purple, often with contrasting spots scattered across the petals. The bright yellow stamens burst from the center of the flower, drawing the attention of pollinators to the garden. These lilies are a favorite for spectacular bouquets from your local florists. Most garden catalogs offer the bulbs that over the years can be divided to share with friends who will remember you each spring as another celebration burst forth from these show-offs.

New England Asters I have not seen these in the nurseries but ordered them from a perennial catalog. Hot, and I do mean hot pink, light pink, blue, white, purple with a yellow center and a shade of magenta I cannot describe, all grace the flower beds of my yard and the ditch behind the house. These plants are very showy,

extremely easy to care for, doing well in sun or shade. Pinching back the branches may encourage the plant to become more bushy. This tough plant does need a little care to get established but will bloom for years. Asters are not good for cutting and seem to have no fragrance.

Bleeding heart The first time I saw this lovely plant was while visiting my daughter at college in Iowa. As soon as I got home I bought it as a "memory plant". They are considered an heirloom plant as they can live for decades. They bloom very early in May,  the stems arching upward with heart-shaped flowers. They prefer deep shade and are a nice addition to the shade garden.

Centranthus (Jupiter Beard) Centranthus are easy to grow, producing tight clusters of little pink or white flowers above narrow green leaves on two-foot stalks. They appreciate full sun and average soil, making them easy for the gardener who doesn't invest a lot of time in flowers.

 **Columbine** Everyone loves the Arizona native columbine! A hardy addition to any garden, columbine prefers the cooler, shaded areas of the yard. The plants spread by seed but are not truly invasive. Could you really have too many? I have had no success with the lovely blue Colorado columbine. A neighbor and I came to the conclusion that it is too dry here. I have also tried other members of the Aquila family in the various shades of reds and yellow and white. They bloom but are out-performed by our native golden columbine.

A couple of years back, I noticed that some pest was stripping the leaves from the stems of the columbine. I took a close look and discovered tiny green worms on the underside of the leaves. I prefer to pick these off but a good insecticide will also finish them. Try to look for something that is natural, not toxic.

Cone flower family
Any flower in this family is wonderful. From the purple and white echinacea to brown-eyed Susan and gloriosa daisy, this is a group that will give a great garden display. They flourish in either

partial shade or full sun with some varieties doing well in the challenging areas of the garden. As a rule, they do not make good cut flowers.

Coreopsis You have probably seen this growing wild. You may have it yourself or know people who do. Confession. I can not get this plant to grow in my yard. I have tried multiple times, seed, plants, nothing works. Sometimes you have to know when to give up. Coreopsis seems to favor the warmer climes around Flagstaff. Fortunately, I'm not the only person who has found this to be true. Once established they re-seed freely and require little care, adding a bright spot to the garden.

Day Lilies My family lived in the Coconino Estates area of Flagstaff as I was growing up, just three miles to the south of where I live now. When I was seven years old, I was walking along the Rio De Flag with some friends. We came upon some day lilies that someone had uprooted and tossed over their back fence. I didn't know what they were at that time. My friends continued their walk but I gathered them all up and took them home. I made a bed for them in the corner of the back yard, digging miniature canals around the plants to keep them well-watered. Over the years, I have learned that this effort was completely unnecessary. Day lilies will grow with out any help at all! From this original clump of day lilies, this is not an exaggeration, there are now hundreds of thousands of day lilies around Flagstaff! You have to work to kill them!

Yet they are a wonderful, beautiful plant. The long narrow leaves come up very early in the spring with the edible flowers blooming on individual stocks the first week in July. The foliage looks good all the way through fall, turning a nice yellow. My original plants were the old native American Lily, which seem to be the hardiest, spreading the fastest. Two new varieties, the small version, Stella d' Oro in yellow and its cousin Little Business in red, are both great. There are whole catalogs devoted to day lilies, all sizes and descriptions, with blooms of white, yellow, salmon, pink, wine, purple, reds and bi-colors. While all of the new varieties are not as hardy as the original, day lilies can afford diminished hardiness. The hybrids are great plants and actually a bit easier to manage.

Daffodils & Tulips I love all spring bulbs but daffodils are definitely my favorite. This is partly because they are hardy and do so well in Flagstaff. While spring bulbs will come back each year without the ground freezing, they seem to bloom better with freezing temperatures during the winter months. Daffodils are good if you live in an area that has deer and elk as the bulbs are toxic. Animals instinctively avoid them. The green leaves and beautiful blossoms of the tulips, on the other hand, are a salad for elk, deer or rabbits. The bulbs provide a tasty treat for chipmunks and squirrels. Tulips are also more sensitive to wind and extreme cold. I do love tulips and since I don't have a problem with wild grazers, I have a few, preferring to concentrate on the daffodils.

Daffodil bulbs can be planted in any exposure, needing very little care. They do benefit from a deep watering before and after they bloom. Plant each bulb four to six inches deep. Mix a little bone meal and manure into the dirt around the bulb, feeding the plant as it blooms. Bone meal is recommended at the time of planting but I have had trouble with neighborhood dogs digging them up because they smelled the bone meal. The bulbs really like sand, so this can be added where they are planted. This offers gardeners a chance to recycle the sand from an old sandbox or construction project.

Never cut the leaves as they are making food for the next year's blooms. They will naturally die back in June with the leaves completely disappearing. Daffodils are great by themselves or in the perennial bed among snapdragons and pansies. Add nasturiums, beans, lettuce or chard to fill in the gaps. The daffodils protect the young seedlings coming up, dying back as the other plants begin to mature, usually by June.

There are over 2,300 varieties of daffodils, from miniatures to large flowered, double, bi and tri-colored or configurations that resembles a butterfly. They make a nice cut flower but need to be placed in a vase by themselves as they are also toxic to other flowers. The bulbs multiply rapidly from year to year. Do not be concerned about the toxicity and danger for household pets. Your dog or cat will avoid them for the same reason other animals do. Children should have no desire to eat them. They don't taste good. I have not heard of a child getting sick from eating a daffodil and that is the worst thing that could happen.

Dividing Bulbs and Perennials

I have often heard people say, "I don't want anything that has to be divided." Honestly nothing HAS to be divided, it CAN be divided. You can leave something for decades and it will still bloom. However, if you want to give some away or add to new beds this is a great way to get new plants. The best time to divide perennials is early spring, as soon as you see them coming up. The bigger the plant, the more difficult to handle and the more stress on the plant.

I usually dig up the whole plant, carefully dividing it into healthy portions. Sometimes roots are so intertwined that you have to take a shovel and cut the root ball in half. I hate doing that, but the plant seems to be fine.

I find moving bulbs is easier when you can see their location EXACTLY. I have driven a shovel through more daffodil bulbs in the fall than I care to consider. All spring bulbs can be moved after they bloom. After dividing the bulbs and replanting, give them a good watering. The leaves may die back after being transplanted, but they will probably bloom the next year.

Delphinium Sometimes referred to as the "queen of the garden", these are beautiful plants that are amazingly hardy. They do better against the house or fence for protection and sometimes need to be staked. They do much better with care and attention. There are new colors now but the old blues are the hardiest. The new varieties may require some root protection during the coldest temperatures of the winter.

Dianthus This family includes carnations, pinks and sweet William, all favorites in a traditional flower garden. The low growing pinks bloom in late spring while the carnations usually grow to one or two feet. The clusters of flowers produced by the sweet William on spikes above the leaves are larger than the single blossoms of the carnation. The pinks don't seem to mind our harsh weather but the sweet William may need winter protection and snow cover if it is to return the following year.

Geraniums This might surprise you but I consider the geranium a perennial because my oldest is twenty-five years old. I always keep them in pots to make them easier to transfer. They are outside all summer and in the house blooming all winter, how can

you beat that? A plant that continually blooms! They come in an array of colors and leaf patterns. They are not prone to pests. They are easy to grow from seed or from cuttings.

During the summer, I place the geraniums in the front yard and along the front of the house. A saucer under each pot ensures an adequate supply of water. A regular dose of plant fertilizer helps them to keep blooming. At the end of the summer, before the first frost, I bring the plants in and cut them back to three or four inches high. To propagate geraniums, make a cut at a 'V' junction on a branch and place the cutting in potting soil in a warm window. Keep the soil lightly moist. Soon a new plant will begin to sprout as roots develop on the cutting. With proper care, geraniums can last for decades.

Hollyhocks This story started thirty years ago. My neighbor, Peter Price, had masses of hollyhocks in his front yard. I had too many baby food jars that had been donated for a craft project. I thought, "I bet I could sell hollyhock seeds at a craft sale in the fall and use up those baby food jars." So, with his permission, I picked a ton of them and filled the baby food jars. And they did sell!

I gave one of the jars to my brother-in-law Dennis who had moved south to the town of Camp Verde and had two acres to fill. He scattered them along a fence and in no time they were everywhere. They were his pride and joy! Every year he would harvest the hollyhock seeds and I would fill more jars. It has been a contest every year to see whether there would be more jars or more seeds!

Last year I was talking to Peter, the original holly-hock source, and he told me that the seeds came from an old homestead in Illinois. As a biologist, he was impressed with the variety of colors at this homestead. I was telling him how many jars we had sold over the years and he burst out laughing. "Well," he said, "that explains it! An out-of-state visitor remarked to him, "There sure are a lot of hollyhocks in Flagstaff!"

Hollyhocks are obviously easy to grow from seed. They don't bloom the first year but you will have them forever, cross pollinating, treating gardeners to new and different colors. They need almost no care, but will grow bigger with water and good soil. A century ago little girls would play wedding with the flowers, using white ones for the bride and colored ones for the wedding party. The opened flowers were the skirts, the buds were the heads and bodice.

Hostas Most gardeners appreciate the showy leaves on the plantain lily with the flower as a bonus. These plants appreciate full shade and a soil rich in compost and a little peat moss. Watch out for slugs that create ugly holes in the foliage. The leaves of the early varieties were a solid green but the new varieties have broad strips of white or yellow on green - very pretty.

Iris Iris are wonderful plants that have proven to be very easy to grow, offering lots of new beautiful colors to experiment with in your garden! They are hardy and long lasting, willing to grow in almost any exposure, as long as they get some sun. They also multiply over time. The gardener may choose to divide the rhizomes as they get crowded.

One big mistake - gardeners often plant them too deep. The top third of the tuber MUST be exposed to the sun in order for them to bloom. It is torture to plant them that way because it seems like they need protection from the harsh winter, but they will do just fine. Force yourself to do it! Think of the rhizome as a turtle sunning itself in the sun. When planting, give the rhizome a scoop of manure and a little sand. Mix half to one cup of bone meal into the dirt around the rhizome. At first the rhizomes require watering every third day but then need less water than other flowers usually receive.

I have found that when you stray from the original iris colors of white, purple and yellow, the plants are not quite as hardy, multiply slower and bloom less. Beautiful as they are in the catalog, all the genetic engineering has it's price!

Lavender or Lavandula The gray-green foliage of lavender adds visual interest to a bed full of dark green plants. Some gardeners love the tiny blossoms for the sweet smell they leave in sachets tucked into fabric packets. The plant appreciates our alkaline soil and requires minimal care, growing in full sun.

Russell Lupine and Wild Lupine Russell Lupine is one of my favorites with beautiful spikes in all sorts of color combinations. The leaves are beautiful and a pretty addition to the perennial bed. I have a special area reserved for them. They like protection and only partial sun. They have an unusual fragrance. Wild blue lupine is easier to grow and while very pretty, the blooms are not quite as showy as the Russell Lupine.

Ox-eye and Shasta Daisies Both of these do very well and are extremely hardy. Ox-eye re-seed, the stems are shorter with smaller flowers blooming in June. Shasta daisies are taller, blooming in July. The Shastas can be plagued by grasshoppers and need to be

cut back after blooming to avoid looking ragged. In recent years, shaggy Shastas have become popular, appearing in many Flagstaff gardens. Both Ox-eye and Shasta daisies do well in full sun to part shade.

Penstemon In Flagstaff it is hard to beat the Rocky Mountain penstemon and a host of other penstemon for a dramatic display. Intense purple stalks bloom in June, creating a stunning roadside display as well as becoming a highlight in local gardens. The plant is extremely hardy, growing almost anywhere. The leaves are attractive and once the bloom stalk is cut remain a nice green ground cover for the rest of the season. They do well in your most difficult area of the yard. Penstemon tend to travel, dropping their seeds for future propagation.

Peony This is another 'memory plant' for me. While camping in Telluride, Colorado in the 80's, I was walking around town and struck up a conversation with an elderly woman who was born and raised in Telluride. She ran the local museum and was a fascinating resource for local history. She had a Victorian garden planted with period flowers around the fence and up the sidewalk of her home. She had several beautiful Peonies with flowers the size of saucers that had a wonderful fragrance. She graciously cut some for me to take to my camp-site. I thought, if they can grow in Telluride at 9,000 feet they can certainly grow in Flagstaff! I have two, one white, the other light pink, both simply beautiful. They seem to like a southern or eastern exposure. Give them plenty of water and fertilizer in the spring for the best blooms.

Phlox There are two main types of phlox and I love them both. The creeping phlox, a ground cover, is beautiful in the spring as it blooms in lavender, hot pink and white. It is extremely hardy and after blooming remains a nice ground cover. The tall phlox is something I have tried more recently. Nurseries carry varieties blooming in blue, lavender, white, pinks and bi colors. The plant is lovely in the garden but I discovered its best virtue only two years ago. I wanted to do a bouquet for a baby shower and I wanted it to be spectacular! So I picked all my phlox as it was blooming. I put it in the living room and the next morning I was  overwhelmed with the wonderful fragrance. I began selling the flower in bouquets on my Farm Stand and people came back looking for the phlox, calling it "that flower that smells so good". So I have been adding to my collection of them. Growing in clumps, they come back bigger each year and are easy to divide for transplant. Some of the new colors are striking! The tall phlox may need to be placed in a protected perennial bed and sometime must be supported with a stake for the first few years.

Setting Boundaries

Sometimes perennial plants do TOO well. They become invasive spread beyond their boundaries. The best thing, if you do like them and want to keep them, is to confine them. Take a one or two gallon black nursery pot. Take the offending perennial, dig it up and put a good portion of it in the pot. Then, bury the pot, with the edge above ground about half inch to an inch. The plant is still part of the garden but has plastic walls confine the spread of the roots underground. The perennial will actually bloom better because it can't put any energy into taking over your flower bed. I did this last year with some bright pink yarrow, artemesia and a variegated grass. I've also confined some members of the campanula family.

California Poppies

California poppies are stunning when a wide swath of the orange blossoms catch the sunlight. They can be difficult to get started and sometimes it is helpful to begin with plants from the nursery, planting them in full sun. They do well at the higher elevation if left undisturbed and allowed to re-seed year after year.

Oriental poppies I planted these in memory of my grandmother who had a large bed of oriental poppies. By the time I reached age 6, and she was close to ninety years of age, the poppies had taken over the entire bed, chasing out any other plants that had been there previously. My neighbor calls them the "prostitutes of the flower world." The blossoms are spectacular when they bloom but

the foliage looks awful most of the year. I spend a lot of time now trying to get rid of the volunteers that emerge when the plants re-seed. If you choose to enjoy the spring display, you might consider cutting back the foliage a month after the blossoms disappear and planting annuals around this perennial.

Salvia Both perennial and annual varieties of salvia make an appearance in high mountain gardens. The perennial variety needs little care other than water and a stake to help keep it upright as it matures. As the stalks show signs of slumping outward, loop a string around the outer circumference of the plant and tie to the stake. Without support, the stalks may slump over neighboring plants.

The annual variety is much better behaved, staying upright. Moist soil and a little winter protection may allow the annual to come back the following year. Both grow in average soil though the plant will benefit from manure and compost.

Scabiosa (Pin Cushion flower) In June, spikes rise out of a low cluster of narrow green leaves to produce tight clusters of flowers, usually not more than two inches in diameter. Bees seem to love these blossoms. In recent years, new varieties have moved beyond the traditional pastels. Scabiosa seems to prefer well-drained alkaline soil in a sunny location.

Sedum Autumn Glory has become very popular in Flagstaff over the last few years as the plants require little care. Sedum actually comes in a number of varieties, from ground cover to the two-foot tall Autumn Glory. While most are easy to identify with fleshy green leaves, the variety 'Dragons blood' turns a bright red. Most varieties have tiny flowers, some of them in eye-appealing clusters. Almost all appreciate a little water now and then though the Autumn sedum seems to take its height from a regular supply of moisture. They provide a nice contrast to annuals and perennials in the garden.

Speedwell / Veronica These are compact little plants that will quietly flourish in either sun or partial shade, requiring little care. The upright spikes of purple flowers go well with yellow columbine. If they begin to outgrow their space in the garden, they are easy to divide and share.

Wood Violet A friend recently complained that her husband told her violets could not grow in Flagstaff. Violets love our mountain-high climate, flourishing without much care. The little purple or white flowers peep from under heart-shaped leaves in the early spring. They prefer a shaded area and are good for rock gardens or as a ground-cover. Many gardeners use them along

borders in front of taller perennials. The clumps expand until gardeners are forced to divide them and wonder where else they can place wood violets, either sun or shade. We sell these in the annual garage sale and people love them as an old-time addition to the garden.

Chrystanthemum
While many of the perennials celebrate spring and summer, the chrysanthemums reign in the fall. They bide their time and as the days begin to grow shorter, the blooms open to give us one last hurrah before winter sets in. The time at which they bloom is governed by the length of our days in the fall.

The local nurseries begin offering mums for sale in the fall and in the following years, the plants grow larger. They can be divided but we must be careful about how deep we plant the roots as they must be at the same level as the original plant. Another method of propagation is to take cuttings from your favorite mum and root them in a commercial potting mix. Take the cutting from the newer growth around the original clump.

I have not had good luck with mums in my garden. I think Cheshire is too cold. I have seen them around town in a wonderful array of colors. They seem to do best on a south or east facing wall, or at least in a location where they are in the sun most of the day. Plant them in a well-amended soil as they are not fond of our heavy clay. Winter protection is recommended.

Rose

Roses do well almost everywhere, providing you choose a variety good for your area. Roses appreciate a moist soil, rich in compost and manure. With our harsh winds, a good fertilizer and a protected location will help them bloom. A controversy has arisen the last few years about how deep to plant a rose with the graft just above or below the soil line. Traditionally, gardeners always kept their graft point above the soil but those in climates experiencing temperatures below 20 degrees argued that it was better to place the graft point below the soil. There was some risk of the plant rotting with

that practice. Recent research shows that placing the graft just above soil level and provide a thick mulch around the plant is sufficient protection from cold winter temperatures. The late fall freeze does not damage the canes and graft point. Instead, it is the deep cold of the early spring storms that may cause the canes to die and turn black. To protect them, a friend recommends cutting the bottom out of a five gallon plastic bucket. Place the bucket over the rose bush and fill with straw. Another local grower suggested wrapping the canes in rags and then piling straw around the plant. Remove the protection in late April, trimming back any dead canes. Fertilize the plant and water generously. As a bloom dies back, trim the branch back to the first sprig with five leaves. Trimming back the dead blossoms is important in encouraging the plant to bloom.

Simplicity, Iceberg and Peace are three good roses for high climates. Miniature roses also do well but may need to come indoors during the winter unless well protected. For a climbing rose you can't beat the old heirloom, Blaze, a bright red rose that I planted at the first house we lived in and it is still there, surviving a variety of home-owners that followed our departure.

 **Yarrow** A very hardy plant, the yarrow is quick to expand into neighboring plants. I've found that if I plant it in a black nursery pot and bury the pot in the garden, the yarrow is better contained. Yarrow likes full sun and will grow in poor soil, an easy plant for beginning gardeners. The feathery, gray foliage is a nice contrast to the bright green of daisies and phlox. Colors range from a cream into yellow and deep red.

Local growers are beginning to expand into a good selection of native plants that require less water to thrive. Russian sage and potentilla, along with penstemon and other favorites, light up our landscapes in the early spring and late summer, reminding us how little effort is required to enjoy God's creation. Check out some of the local selection and imagine how you can give them a place of honor in your garden.

~ Perennial Vines ~

Akebia I hesitate to include this plant as it has been declared invasive in five eastern states. Local gardeners have introduced it to their lots, maintaining a close watch to see if it will spread. Akebia will spring up a trellis on a northern exposure however a sunny exposure will bring out the small pink flowers.
Semi-evergreen, -25 degrees.

Clematis Each year growers introduce new shades and varieties of this garden favorite. Driving around Flagstaff, the old varieties are spectacular, draped over fences and climbing sunny walls. The secret to growing clematis is keep the leafy top of the vine in sun while shading the roots. Try planting some nice annuals around the roots. The vine appreciates a well composted soil and regular watering, repaying the grower by climbing to eight feet or more in height, covered with a rich carpet of blossoms in late June.
Deciduous, -20/-25 degrees.

Honeysuckle Tubular pink flowers that draw hummingbirds make this a popular vine with gardeners. Honeysuckle may take a couple of years to get established before beginning to climb.
Evergreen, -20 degrees.

Ivy Not all gardeners appreciate the enthusiasm of ivy to scale rock walls and spread across walkways. The vine is fairly easily controlled and creates a lovely accent on a bare wall. Ivy does well in full sun but will tolerate some shade. Evergreen, -20 degrees.

Pyracantha (Fire Thorn) You don't want to fall into this woody vine or the thorns may leave their mark on tender skin as many children have discovered. The vine can either climb a chain link fence or fill out as a free-standing shrub. In the spring, pyracantha has beautiful white blossoms that form clusters of red berries in late summer. You may need to trim the woody vine back as it matures over the years to keep a nice shape and encourage new growth. Some garden guides classify this plant as able to tolerate  temperatures down to zero degrees but we have many long-lived plants around Flagstaff that have survived a drop to - 20 degrees. Evergreen.

Virginia Creeper We all love the red foliage of Virginia Creeper in the fall as it hangs from the side of buildings and along fences. Once it gets established however, the creeper wants to take over everything, invading prime garden space and shutting out sunlight from plants in its shade. Where once I welcomed the vine, I am now removing it to encourage other plants to climb the chain link in my back yard. The roots are invasive and removing it may become a multi-year project. Think carefully before welcoming this vine into your garden. The vine seems to prefer full sun but can still spread into shady areas where it loves moist soil. Deciduous, Down to -40 degrees.

Silver Lace This fast-growing vine will tolerate some shade but flowers more freely in a sunny location. Clusters of tiny white flowers give it a delicate appearance with the vine doing well on a trellis, framing the entrance to a garden. Gardeners will need to periodically cut back the vine as it tends to branch out, seeking new supports.
Deciduous, Tolerates -20/-25 degrees.

Note: Temperature toleration is based on varieties suited to this climate.

~ Plant Sources ~

How do you obtain all these great plants without taking out a loan? Start with one garden bed at a time. Then, ask a gardener to share! If you have a friend who has a plant you want, ask to trade one of yours or ask for a division. Most gardeners with established gardens are happy to do this as they need to thin out their own plants anyway. Our local church, Flagstaff Christian Fellowship, sponsors a large garage sale every year with a selection of perennials for sale. Local people put it on their calendars, knowing they can buy plants that are already acclimated to our soil and climate. Sometimes driving around town, I am reminded of our FCF garage sale! If you don't have generous gardening friends, arrange a plant exchange in your neighborhood. Not only will you possibly obtain new varieties of plants, but you will come to know your neighbors.

For hard to find plants there are great catalogs to choose from or your local nursery may be able to help. I suggest that when purchasing from a nursery, buy the smallest size available and carefully nurture it into a garden trophy. The bigger the plant, the more expensive! Most nurseries put their perennials on sale in the late summer, so this is a good time to buy and a good time to plant.

Keep a sharp watch around your neighborhood. I have often found plants being discarded, just like the day I found the day lilies when I was seven. On one occasion, I found over 200 daffodils bulbs left by the side of the road. Last year I was walking to the park and a neighbor was digging up her tulips. She had a huge pile of pink tulips bulbs. When I walked back home, I stopped and asked what she was going to do with them. She replied, "Throw them out! I don't like pink!" I took them home! I love pink.

Bulbs can be expensive but they all go on sale at the end of the season, usually late November, December and even January. You may find great deals at this time with bulbs at least 50%

There are many ways to cut the price of plants but treat yourself to at least one new plant at FULL PRICE each year!

off, sometimes more. When purchasing very late, the ground may be frozen so I have grown them indoors the first season. Oh, what glory to have daffodils blooming in February in the house! I plant them in a pot at least 10 inches deep, with only the bottom one third of the bulb in the soil. This leaves almost the entire pot for the roots. You can also layer them for a spectacular display. This works well when you have so many bulbs in your yard you are not quite sure where there is an open space to plant them. Your daffodils grown indoors will die down before the ones in your garden, allowing you to easily move these new bulbs to open spaces in your yard in anticipation of the next year. I have over 1,000 daffodils in my yard and alley. My estimated cost for these over the years is under fifty dollars!

Chapter 7

BEST ANNUALS
for the MOUNTAINS OF THE SOUTHWEST

If perennials are so great why even bother with annuals? Good question! Annuals bloom all summer! Their profuse, spectacular displays with vibrant color add so much to your yard. Many gardeners use the cut flowers in bouquets or munch on those that are edible. Some of the easiest flowers to start outdoors include marigolds and zinnias as their seeds are large enough to handle easily.

If you visit a local nursery, you will find annuals sold either as seed packets or six packs. You'll note that there seems to be a much greater diversity of perennials. I've chosen to include annuals that seem to do the best in our challenging climate and so I recommend them. The diversity within each family grants us a wide variety to add a bright splash of color to our favorite perennials. Once the frost comes, the annuals are history until we plant our favorites again next year.

When planting your flowers remember that blues and purple shades tend to disappear in the landscape. Keep them close to the front door paths or sidewalk so you can enjoy them. Hot shades like yellows pinks and reds jump out from almost anywhere.

I will start with the annuals I find the hardiest, blooming first in the season.

Sweet Peas I grew sweet peas, an old favorite, for my wedding bouquet. Just like the delicious snap peas, sweet peas can be started very early as they are frost proof and need a wire fence

to climb. Some of the newer varieties have had that wonderful aroma bred out of them, so if you want fragrance, look for the old varieties. Soak the seeds for 24 hours and plant fairly close together. Don't mix sweet peas with edible peas as the sweet pea pods are toxic or poisonous for humans. The pods look different, but it is still not worth taking a chance.

Pansy Family Pansies, including violas and johnny jump ups, are cold hardy and fun to look at with those cute little faces. The edible blossoms are perfect for salads, vegetable or fruit trays  and desserts. Gardeners grow them for their culinary uses if nothing else. Different colors have different tastes. They are often the first to emerge each spring, peeping through the snow showers. Many gardeners find that their pansies die out when the warm weather settles in.

I've found that pansies planted on the south side of a house can bloom till December. They often come up a second year. Johnny Jump-ups will re-seed and often last for years popping up all over the yard. This year for the first time I tried planting violas from seed and now have a nice mix of colors to enjoy.

Snapdragons Another cold hardy plant, snapdragons are easy to care for and produce loads of blooms all summer and well into fall. They are great in bouquets or by themselves, they tolerate shade well and will even last two years or more if they are planted in a protected place. I had two pots full of snapdragons last summer that I have been over-wintering in a back room. They are doing great and I  think I will get another productive season from them.

Seeds or Six-Packs?

(We're not talking six packs of beer!)

Some gardeners find it best to start their annuals indoors. The seeds of annuals need to be planted in soil that has been warmed by the sun. With such a short growing season in our mountain region, waiting for the soil to reach optimum temperature may be a waste of precious growing time. Some gardeners, planting before optimum temps, find that their seeds have rotted as they diligently struggled to keep the top layer of soil moist.

So save your empty six-pack seedling containers from plants you purchased the previous year and fill them half way with potting soil or, if you're really particular, a seedling medium. Drop your seeds into each little pocket of planting medium and mist thoroughly with a spray bottle. If you can, keep them in a warm place as you wait for the seeds to germinate. Keep them moist but not so wet that the seed rots. As the seedlings begin to appear and sprout upwards, you can add extra potting soil to each container, helping to support the fragile seedling. In time, you can begin watering as you would any other plant.

An alternative to starting your own seedlings is to visit your local nursery. If you have a lot of space set aside for annuals, this can get pricey. If you are using the annuals as highlights mixed with your perennials, then this may be a good option for you. Some gardeners hate to spend the time nursing tiny seedlings along as they wait for outside temperatures, both air and soil, to warm. Again, a visit to a local nursery may be the preferable alternative.

Marigolds Marigolds are easy to grow and they come in all sizes with different configurations on their petals. They help deter some garden pests and they are easy for kids to grow. I don't like them. I don't like how they look and I don't like how they smell. The same lady who was pulling out her entire bed of pink tulips has a yard full of them. She likes yellow and orange. I have to admit her yard is pretty and very festive. Check the garden catalogs for a greater variety than what is found in your local nursery.

Zinnas are a great flower! There are several varieties from the Lilliput with half inch blossoms to the giants sporting a nice cutting flower that can be up five inches across. Flower varieties include the cactus with narrow petals to the more traditional

look with stripped and speckled broad, flat petals. I have always grown them, planting the seed directly into the ground. I think they would do better if started inside and then put out. They need a longer growing season with like rich soil and as much warmth as you can provide.

Petunias Nothing is as spectacular as a pot or basket of petunias! Several years ago I was visiting my daughter in Indiana. We drove the entire length of the state through small towns, looking at farms and a few cemeteries, making a perfect day for me! The highlight was when we stopped at an Amish nursery. The owner's home was right next door and hanging from the second story was a plant that LOOKED like a petunia but it was hanging down about four feet and literally had 500 blooms on it. I asked, "What is that?"

The woman replied, "It's a petunia. I planted it from seed in February. The secret is to water every day and give it Miracle-Gro every two weeks."

There you have it, the secret of growing petunias! I tried her advice that summer and sure enough they were the best petunias I had ever grown. They also make a great border for taller perennials, adding a bright splash of color.

Impatiens These low growing plants are great in the shade, their blossoms brightening subdued shady beds. As they grow, the foliage seems to hug the borders of the bed, mounding over rocks and edging. I would probably  recommend buying these from your local nursery well after the last frost as they are very tender. Keep an eye out for garden pests that like to munch on the tender stems. In Arizona, as our monsoons move in mid-July, the impatiens seem to explode, making them a favorite for gardeners. Try them with annual salvia and alyssum.

 **Cosmos** Cosmos are fun to grow from seed, creating a tall display of graceful, green foliage with bright blossoms. They are hardy in areas where other flowers might not do well. They make a great cut flower and look especially nice mixed in with vegetables or as a backdrop to spring bulbs. They easily re-seed and return the next year. They are super easy to transplant.

Nasturiums This is another tasty flower, although spicier than the pansy family. They are easy to plant with large seeds and easy to grow in poor soil. The circular leaves add visual interest and the

59

flowers make a very nice fresh bouquet. They are thought to be a deterrent to insects. In Flagstaff, they don't start blooming profusely till August. Some varieties of nasturiums stand six inches tall while others climb trellises as vines.

Sunflowers One snowy, winter day in January I was thumbing through my seed catalogs and decided to call a nursery with a question about a variety of squash. The woman who answered the phone didn't know the answer and asked, "Would you like to speak to our resident farmer?"

"Sure," I said. What she couldn't see was how I rolled my eyes and shook my head while thinking, they don't have a resident farmer. When Jeff Werner answered the phone I asked, "So, I understand you're a farmer."

"I am," he replied. "I had a 500 acre organic farm. It's smaller now but still keeps me busy. I sell my produce at a Farmers Market."

I could not believe my good fortune. A grower who sells his produce and knows both ends of the business. I hit him with a barrage of questions and gained so much valuable information. He was an incredible resource. Two hours later he was able to escape my phone call. He told me he could only talk that long in the slow months. In the conversation, I asked what flowers he sold at the Farmers market. He said sunflowers were the number one seller and his favorite was the top selling sunflower, a bi-color from Harris Seed called Pro-cut Bi-color.

"I don't get it with sunflowers," I said. "I see customers buying them at the local Farmers Market but why do people buy them?"

"They make people happy," he answered.

Okay, that was a good reason. I ordered a package of 250 seeds. For some reason, I went for broke and planted the whole package. I had never grown a sunflower and wasn't sure what they would need or what they would do. I planted them all over the front and back yard, the side yard, in pots, close together, far apart, good soil, poor soil, even transplanted them to see how they would fare. They were great fun! The seedlings came up well, grew quickly and started to bloom. All the blooms faced the street like they were showing off.

People stopped their cars to look at sunflowers. People brought their cameras and were taking pictures, asking for seed for the next year. The cut flowers sold like crazy. Sunflowers, I thought, do make people feel happy. They are making ME happy!

This variety bloomed relatively early in August. The incredibly strong stems stood erect and did not need to be staked for support. The plants produced one giant flower and then additional smaller blooms on the same stem. I found that even the plants in poor soil, part shade or too close together produced a nice size flower that sometimes was more manageable than the giants produced by ideal conditions. I found they last a long time, up to two weeks, either in the yard or as a cut flower. Sunflowers are an excellent flower for children to try.

Decorative Dahlias Do you love the elegance of dinner-plate dahlias but wonder how to grow them with our short growing season? Here's a couple of idea from other gardeners. Dahlias love compost-rich, well-drained soil in full sun. A friend's grand-mother used to add three shovelfuls of manure to the  hole when planting the tubers. Add a little bone meal to feed the plant as it blooms. When she watered, she was careful to give each mature plant a long, slow drink and staked the heavy stems as they began to inch upward. In our shorter growing season, some gardeners prefer to raise the larger dahlias in deep pots so that they can bring them inside when the first frosts wipe out the garden. To grow the largest flowers, consider pinching off the side shoots in order to encourage one blossom that will grow to the size of a dinner plate. As the plants get taller, you may need to gently loop a string, tying the stalk to the support.

To store the tubers, cut the stems back to about six inches above ground level after the first frost. Loosen the soil very carefully around the tubers and lift from the ground, carefully removing any soil clinging to the roots. Take care not to damage or remove the old stems. Hang the tubers upside down for a couple of weeks to allow them to dry then tuck them away in a cool, dry place till spring. Some gardeners sprinkle sulfur on the tubers to protect them from fungus. Do not store the tubers when damp as they will rot.

Mike and Sarah Cromer grow some beautiful dahlias every year, winning blue ribbons at our county fair. In the fall, Mike enjoys sharing his dinner-plate dahlias with some of their older friends who no longer have gardens of their own.

In the spring, start the tubers in pots. Watering sparingly as you do not want the tuber to rot before the early shoots appear above the soil line.

~ Annuals In Containers ~

Many of our annuals make a great display in containers, placed around the entrance to a home or along a sunny deck. Two favorites that are strangers to our freezing temperatures are heliothorpe and lantana. We see a lot of lantana in landscaping in the deserts of Arizona. The clusters of red, yellow and orange flowers are brilliant when lit by the sun.

The rich purple clusters of heliotrope are scented with a wonderful vanilla fragrance. The dark green foliage is an attractive contrast to so many of the annuals that this plant is quickly becoming a favorite in our area as well. Other container favorites include shade-loving wax begonias and coleus along with the dark leaves of the sweet potato vine. Impatiens and pansies are great container plants as well. Consider arranging these in stair-stepping levels to enhance the entrance to any home.

Grouping plants and pots together is very attractive and draws your eyes to that arrangement. You can hide black pots or other unattractive pots by staggering and layering other pots in front of them to make a mass of blooms. I have done this on the top of my driveway and it really is nice to look at! It is easier to water that way as well. The arrangement has a more artistic look than

placing them in a row. Occasionally I have a bouquet from some event or a plant that I was transplanting. I put the flowers in a vase and tuck them in the yard somewhere, creating 'illusional gardening'. Very nice!

~ Annual Vines ~

Black-eyed Susan Transplants from the mid-west know and love the black-eyed Susan vine. Unlike the perennial cone flowers, these vines quickly climb to cover a drab wall or plain terrace, displaying gold or orange blossoms, each with the signature dark center. Placed on a sunny southern exposure, in the late afternoon the blossoms turn to living gold, lighting up the  garden. Unlike the plumbago, this vine should not be brought inside to escape the cold temperatures. Instead, either start it from seed in early April or plan to purchase the vine - if you can find it before other gardeners snap it up at your local nursery.

 **Plumbago** This is a new vine for me. A friend introduced me to this woody climber that has tight clusters of blue blooms, resembling a miniature hydrangea. In our climate, plumbago is an annual. She trims it back, digs it up in the fall and repots it, bringing the plant indoors. Even when a light frost gets to the plant before she does, the plant seems to rebound with regular watering and survives till it can return outside the following summer. Plumbago appreciates a sunny wall, slightly acidic, sand soil with regular watering. The narrow leaves and woody stalks may need to be encouraged as a vine. The blue clusters of flowers are just lovely, making the effort worthwhile.

Chapter 8

BEST VEGETABLES
FOR FLAGSTAFF & THE MOUNTAIN SOUTHWEST

There is nothing more satisfying in this world (except raising children), than growing a vegetable from seed and eating the fruit of your labor. I still remember jumping out of bed as a five-year-old to run outside to see if the squash were coming up. After 50 years, it is still a thrill to see the little squash seedling poking through the dark earth. Many of the problems that people experience in growing vegetables are self-imposed. Remember three simple things.

> 1) No region in the world has "perfect conditions" for growing everything. Everyone faces an obstacle in growing annuals and vegetables. Pests vary from one place to another. Conditions are too wet or too dry, too cool or too hot. The soil may be poor. We all have our challenges!
> 2) Concentrate on the vegetables suited for your area. Ninety percent of your vegetables should be things that thrive where you live. It is okay to have some fun and experiment, but failure isn't fun. Crop failure can be too common when we try things that aren't suited to our area. You can't grow everything!
> 3) Learn from your mistakes! Every year is another opportunity to learn something new. No experience is ever lost, so with an attitude to learn, you can reap great benefits year after year. When something doesn't do well, ask yourself why. Do I need to improve the soil, try a different exposure, change how I water or use a different variety?

~ How Do You Determine What To Grow? ~
Start by observing what grows well in your neighborhood. As

65

you walk through your neighborhood, if you notice a lot of a particular variety of plant, this indicates that this plant does well in your area! Vegetables are more difficult to observe because often they are in the back yard. Gardeners LOVE to talk about their gardens, what they grow and what has done well for them. Begin by engaging experienced gardeners in conversations. Generally, they will be happy to share their experience with you. Local nurseries can be helpful as well as master gardeners in your area. Western states have a county extension office with expert advice. The internet has become a great resource for the home gardener. However, nothing beats personal experience for learning and understanding the preference of a particular vegetable.

I will start with a discussion of cold weather veggies and move to the warmer ones.

Snap Peas Delicious snap peas should be in every garden! Make use of our cool weather with these little treasures! I plant my snap peas along both a chain link fence and against a solid wood fence covered with wire in the back yard. This is one of the coldest areas of my yard and the peas love it! Provided there is not two feet of snow on the ground, I plant in mid-March, sowing  thickly in two rows. I soak my peas for 24 hours before planting. This helps offset the difficulties in keeping the soil moist. They are not fazed by freezing nights and continue to grow. Usually they climb the fence by themselves but sometimes they need a little help. I either help them curl around the wire or if they are really stubborn, I use a twist tie to secure them.

In mid summer they take a "break" when it gets warm. Keep watering as they will resume blooming and produce peas till frost. When well watered, the vines may top a six-foot chain link fence. They do very well in part shade. There are a number of varieties but I use 'Sugar Snap' from Harris seeds.

Lettuce Lettuce is another hardy vegetable that does extremely well in cool weather but tends to bolt in the heat. You can direct sow into the soil or you can sow thickly in a smaller container and transplant to get a more even distribution. Lettuce transplants very easily. Most seed companies now have a lettuce

mix or you can make your own mix in ordering several favorite varieties. I DID NOT LIKE the mesclun mix as some of the greens were too strong and 'biting'. The LETTUCE mix contains only lettuce and is DELICIOUS. With a mix we are able to try a nice variety of different lettuce, all beautiful to look at in the salad bowl. Don't forget to add your violas and nasturtiums!

Remember, to plant a second crop later in the season as that planted in March or April will not live through September. (T&E) July 1st is an ideal date for a second planting. To harvest, I never pull my lettuce up with the roots. Instead, give it a haircut, leaving at least a couple of inches on the plant to sprout new leaves. You can do this numerous times throughout the season. Another option is to just pick the outside leaves, efficient but time-consuming. Lettuce does well in containers and tolerates part shade. I recommend the lettuce mix from Pinetree Seeds, their most popular selection. The one ounce package is the best value.

Cabbage My grandmother loved growing cabbage in her half-block farm in downtown Flagstaff. She became well-known for her little cabbages.

Cabbage / Dave Menne's garden

In the early 1900's, families were often large and cabbage became a staple in their diet. Cabbage could be stored easily without refrigeration in root cellars through the winter.

My grandmother was familiar with the requirements for growing cabbage due to her early years growing up on a farm in Sweden. Cabbage became a popular American vegetable, unlike her beloved rutabagas which she grew and fed to her six children. There wasn't much of a market for rutabagas. My grandmother started cabbage in a cold frame and then moved it out into the garden when summer arrived. I find it very beautiful and highly nutritious. Cabbage needs good soil and full sun.

Kale I first tried to grow Kale due to a request from a Farmstand customer. Despite crop failure over the first three years, I become more successful with each year. I've learned from my failures about how the plant grows and what it requires in the garden. I continue to work with a heirloom variety called Red Russian. It is a lovely blue green, frilled, leafy plant with purple edging and veins. The first time I took a bite of it I thought, "Good grief, who is eating this, other than the insects?" I have found though that as I nibble it from time to time I am growing to really like it. Kale is an acquired taste. The Olive Garden restaurant serves a popular, delicious soup which uses kale as one of the main ingredients.

I've learned, T&E, that kale looks like a "tough" plant but is needy, particularly when young. Give kale a lot of sun, manure and compost with consistent, deep watering. The plants need a lot of room as they grow very large so pay attention to spacing, giving them eighteen inches between plants.

Like I mentioned earlier, the bugs go for kale in a big way. Protect the seedlings and carefully watch the plants throughout the season. Slugs will mow it down. Look for them at night or "bait" them with something they like, then "harvest" them. Black corn fleas seem to have radar fixed on kale and can quickly decimate a plant. Grasshoppers will devour them as well. I'm surprised at how insects prefer kale over any other vegetable in my garden, even lettuce. They must know kale is one of the most nutritious vegetables on the planet! After all, kale kept many people alive during the hardships of World War I and II.

Harvest the plant by cutting the outer leaves. The taste improves after a light frost and can be harvested long after everything else is gone. Most people prefer it cooked, used in soups and stews. The internet is a great source for recipes.

Swiss Chard is delightful to grow and is a great vegetable for cold weather!

I use several varieties. The White chard grows the fastest but the Northern Lights or Rainbow chard is so beautiful, it has to be included! Again, soak the seeds before planting. Chard will not tolerate partial shade like lettuce but requires more sun.

The large seeds are easy to direct sow. I was driven nuts the first year wondering why three plants emerged so close together. I knew I didn't plant them that close. The seeds are actually in a pod, containing from one to four seeds! Don't worry about thinning them too much. After a good watering, pull any plants up just like a weed. Thin the leaves and plant in another bed.   Chard transplants very well even at four to five inches high.

Tyfon-Holland Greens

I first learned of Tyfon-Holland Greens through the Pinetree Garden catalogue. The description read, "If you want to feed an army from a garden the size of a coffee table, this might be the vegetable for you." I thought that description was indeed for me! My customers describe the taste as a mild version of mustard greens and they LOVE it. I am extremely pleased with the Holland greens and often harvest in self defense as I watch them grow at a frightening rate. The seedlings need a little extra care when young but once established seem indestructible. The insects don't seem to be drawn to this variety as they are to Kale or Chard. I was going to try Mustard and collard greens but have decided to stick with the Holland greens. A true green connoisseur could try a wide variety to see what they liked best.

You can begin harvesting whenever you want by cutting the outer leaves, taking care not to cut the interior stalk.

Chard is delicious both raw and cooked, using many great recipes available on the internet. Most people saute it with garlic or onions, or in just a little olive oil. Fifty percent of my Farm Stand customers had never tried chard before but they love it now! Don't allow the chard to get as big as seen in the produce section or Farmers market. I like to cut it at eight to ten inches and the  plants can be harvested all season. The white chard comes back the second year. I use it in the early spring and then, as it goes to seed, I pull it out and plant something else.

Spinach Spinach thrives in cold weather and is super easy to grow. Some gardeners have seen the spinach they planted the previous fall, emerge in the spring as the snow melts away. Again, the seeds are easy to handle - plant directly.

Summer Squash My favorite vegetable is summer squash as I love watching it grow. The seeds can be directly sewn outdoors in the spring once the danger of frost is past. I need it sooner for my Farm Stand so I start the plants indoors. I soak the seeds overnight or for 24 hours and then place them in a shallow tray filled with potting soil,  barely covering them. They go behind the wood-burning stove or the warmest place you can find. They germinate very quickly in two to four days. As soon as each seed begins to germinate, I transplant it to a quart-size pot. These pots are filled with a mix of good compost and manure with a little perlite or potting soil to lighten it. In transplanting to the pots, I ensure that every pot has a plant growing in it.

My absolute favorite variety is Zucchini Elite from Harris seeds. This is a perfect squash plant as it produces loads of nice straight zucchini and grows straight up. The plant resembles a zucchini tree, allowing me to walk between the rows. I also like other varieties such as the yellow straight neck and crook neck which is especially good as baby squash. They are so flavorful. I'm very pleased with Golden Rod, a yellow zucchini from Harris Seeds, that I've tried for the first time this year. The squash is the deepest yellow I have ever seen and a vigorous producer.

I love the original zucchini, Cocozelle, because it is HUGE. As it does spread, I like to place it in areas where spreading is not a problem. There is a lovely pale green variety called Dali, also known as a Lebanese or Mediterranean squash. I like mixing all these colors and types on my Farm Stand.

You will notice in the seed catalogues novelty squashes,

round zucchinis, two tone squash, etc. Remember as in some of the perennial plants, altering the genetics to achieve different shapes and colors weakens the overall plant. You won't get the same yield and hardiness as you would in the more tried and true varieties.

Summer squash is a needy vegetable! They require full sun with lots of organic material especially manure. They also need lots of water on a consistent schedule. They are extremely frost sensitive. To ensure continued production, keep picking the squash. In northern Arizona the plants seem to do better when they are surrounded with black plastic. I have even used black fabric to warm their roots.

Two years ago, I visited a garden in Taylor, Arizona. This elderly man had converted his entire front yard to vegetables, with a small flower garden on the side. It was beautiful. I told him I had come all the way from Flagstaff to see his garden! It made his day. His wife, wondering why he had not come in for lunch, came out looking for him. He told her, "She came all the way from Flagstaff to see my garden!" His wife looked at him in total disbelief and said, "She did not!" I assured her that indeed, this was true. This man was a wealth of information! He showed me the benefit of black plastic mulch, saying that he used it every year on his squash, giving him a huge advantage. As soon as I got home I put black "anything", including plastic and fabric, around my squash plants. Last year I placed black plastic around almost every squash and had the best production so far. The plants that didn't have it were half the size of those that did, all other things being equal.

Winter Squash, Pumpkins & Gourds

Next to summer squash, the winter squash and pumpkins are my favorite! The growing conditions are almost the same summer squash but winter squash are hardier than their summer cousins. They can tolerate more shade, less water and poor soil. Gardeners have an advantage in leaving the winter squash for harvesting till the end of the season after the frost has nipped  the leaves. They keep for months, allowing the gardener to eat them during the cold months when all else is gone.

The vines of the winter squash love to roam all over the place, climbing fences, growing over the driveway or stretching across the lawn. Give them room to grow. When I am starting a new area that is covered with weeds and the soil has not been improved, one hill with winter squash can hide the weeds!

Gourds are fun to grow. I have noticed a distinct difference between the sexes in their reaction to the gourds. EVERY woman says, "Oh look at those cute little gourds. They are so pretty." EVERY man looks intently at them, studies them and says, "Can you eat them?" When I say no,

I can see their curiosity getting the best of them. They ask, "Why do you grow them?" As gourds are not edible, I use fertilizer in growing the gourds to enormous lengths - just for fun.

Beans At one time the predominate vegetable crop grown in Flagstaff was beans, not green beans but pinto beans. The neighborhoods now known as Upper Greenlaw, Doney Park and much of Sunnyside were bean fields. Beans do well in Flagstaff!

Bush beans have a short growing season. The plants are extremely sensitive to frost and very hard to cover. As they need warm air and warm soil to germinate, I plant them in mid-June. (T&E) They can tolerate part shade and be tucked here and there in the corners of your garden. They can be planted where daffodils or other bulbs are just dying back, grouped or put in rows. They add nitrogen to the soil so they are beneficial, as are peas, to the garden.

My favorite place to plant them is in "hose guard pots" placed strategically to keep my hose in line. You can use these pots for lots of things but beans are very good. Planted in pots, the beans are much easier to pick, they don't get dirty, or have slugs and other pests eating them. (I hate that). When I have compost that is not fully decomposed, I fill the lower 80 percent of the pot with compost, the top 20 percent with good soil. By the time the beans are finished producing for the season the lower eighty percent is beautifully decomposed.

Pole beans are fun to grow, they taste great and they are easy to pick. I love pole beans! As their name implies, they need a pole. They do not like chain link fence, the diamond-shaped links confuse them. You can use a trellis or sturdy string tied to a fence. I have used stakes, poles and "wedding arbors" purchased at garage sales. The pole beans grow up the sides of the arbor but never extend across the center bars. The vines usually don't need help attaching to the trellis but if they do, remember they wind around the support counter-clockwise. In order to get the best harvest you need to plant pole beans in mid to late May. They will produce till frost. Since they are usually in a more confined area, they are a little easier to cover if a late frost descends on the garden.

Tomatoes
The best place for tomatoes in Flagstaff is next to the house, on the east or south side of your home. They like to be in a five gallon or larger **BLACK** pot to warm their roots. In some of the warmer areas of town, friends have success growing tomatoes directly in their gardens.

Four things tomatoes love:
good compost, heat, water, protection.

Four things tomatoes hate:
wind, cold, sporadic watering, hard rain & hail.

Planting
In May, take your well watered plant (purchased or grown from seed), clip leaves along the stem, not too close, leaving the top leaves intact. Gently turn the pot over and let the plant slide out. Bury as far down in either the five gallon pot or the ground as possible, leaving the top leaves above

soil line. If planted in pots, the pot should be deeper than it is wide. Gently fill the holes with the best soil available. I prefer a combination of compost, manure and good soil. Water several times in the process. The stem will quickly root where you have clipped the branches, creating a two-tier set of roots.

After filling the hole, place a sturdy (large size) tomato cage around the plant, sinking the tines into the soil. For extra support, a wood or metal stake can go along the edge of the pot. Water daily. Using a clothespin or clip, secure a sheet over the back of the plants next to the house. One sheet will cover 4-5 plants. Uncover the plants in the morning, cover again at night as long as there is a threat of frost. I prefer to continue doing this till mid-June to give the plants extra warmth. I

sometimes leave them covered for several days at a time during a cold snap or with high winds. Unfortunately, this is not uncommon in Flagstaff during May or June.

For a VERY hard freeze use crumpled newspaper or cotton rags around the stem. Add a cloth over the interior lower rung of the cage, with an additional sheet or light blanket on top. You can also use a string of Christmas lights along the cages for added warmth. I don't use 'walls of water' but many people swear by them. Try them and see how you like them. They actually can remain on the plant for an entire season.

I sing a little good night song to them in the evening while covering and good morning song to begin their day. Singing to your tomatoes is optional! In no time, with a little extra care, you will have a robust tomato plant!

Seed
There are wonderful varieties to choose from that the nurseries don't carry. Catalogues classify tomatoes as either determinate or indeterminate.

Determinate = compact
Indeterminate = large, climbing & spreading

Considering our short growing season, select a variety with a maturation or growing season no longer than 70 days. It is fun and very rewarding to grow your tomatoes from seeds. If started early, you can have a good sized, hearty plant in May! I plant the seeds as early as January 1st. Consider planting by Valentines Day as a deadline if you want mature plants for your mountain garden by May.

How to plant tomato seeds:
Using a quart-size pot or slightly smaller, fill with good compost mixed with a little perlite or potting soil to lighten the planting compound. Place pot(s) in a plastic tray, storage box, hospital wash basin etc. Water thoroughly, leaving the mix damp. Follow directions on the seed packet. I use a pencil to make an indentation. I plant two seeds per pot about a quarter inch apart. Sometimes only one comes up, but if both are hearty, I let them both grow. If you are trying several varieties, mark them with plant markers. As heat rises, place the tray in the warmest spot in the house: behind the wood burning stove, near the dryer or on a shelf. Remember to keep them moist. The seedlings take about a week to emerge. As soon as the first one is up, move it or the whole tray to your warmest, sunniest window. They will remain there until they are planted. They may need a bit of liquid fertilizer while in the window. If they become long and leggy, pinch back each branch to help produce a thick, sturdy stem.

Buying Plants
I recommend nursery plants for novice gardeners for the first two years. The bigger the plant, the more expensive. Avoid the varieties that require a longer maturation like Beef Steak and Big Boy. With our short growing season, you'll

have better results with tomatoes that require about 60 days to maturation. Some of my favorites include Early Girl, Sweet 100 cherry or a bush Goliath.

After planting, remove the blossoms on the smaller tomato plants so the plant will concentrate the nutrients it receives toward growing.

Tips For increased production, brush tomato blossoms with a child's paintbrush or Q-tip.

If you are growing tomatoes in pots, recognize that even with the best intentions, pots dry out. You will notice the soil pulling away from the edge of the pot. Don't quickly dump a gallon of water into the pot as the water will run straight through. Pour a gallon, one cup at a time, s-l-o-w-l-y onto the tomatoes to allow it to rehydrate. It may require two to three gallons.

If the frost catches your tender plants before all the tomatoes have ripened, pick the green fruit and either lay it out on newspaper or store in a paper bag. The tomatoes will continue to ripen off the vine. Check the tomatoes every day, using them as they ripen.

To the first person who said "Pull up your tomatoes and hang them in the garage", I would like to hunt them down and make them clean up the mess in thousands of garages across America. I would force them to eat pithy tomatoes with skins as tough as leather.

PICK ALL YOUR TOMATOES, PLACE THEM IN A BOX. THEY WILL RIPEN QUICKLY AND BE DELICIOUS! For the smallest green tomatoes, check out the recipes on the internet for green fried tomatoes. Again delicious!

The Good News and Bad News about Root Crops

Let's define root crops, these are any crop with the primary vegetable growing underground. This includes beets, turnips, garlic, onions, parsnips, rutabagas, carrots and potatoes.

First the GOOD news. Root crops are very cold hardy. They can be planted early and harvested late. We need not worry about covering or protecting them from frost. That is good news for mountain gardeners! They are relatively pest free and easy to grow. They also will tolerate part shade, another positive point. With beets and turnips, we get a bonus as the green leafy tops of these plants are delicious.

Now the BAD news: The very fact that they are growing four to ten inches deep under ground is a serious problem when you are dealing with poor soil. As I mentioned in the section on soil, in Flagstaff we have "various forms of rock" rather than soil. Compost will certainly solve the problem, but that requires a lot of compost or manure! Best to save the compost for the high maintenance plants. I have found sand is helpful in loosening the soil and is very inexpensive. Pick up a load from your local building material supplier or order a good amount from the local "dirt guy". After he dumps a pile at the end of your driveway, you can deliver the amount you need with a wheelbarrow to the correct spot. If you have children or grandchildren, you can use some for a sandbox. Maybe a neighbor or two would like to go in on a load as they plan their home projects, using the sand to cushion pavers in their landscaping.

Most people don't realize horse radish is a root crop. The root can be very hard on your hands and eyes when preparing it so take precautions.

Be sure to follow nursery directions for

starting seed potatoes. Other root crops are started from seed, following standard guidelines. If planted too closely, you may need to thin the seedlings to allow the survivors room to develop.

~ Novelty Crops ~

I call these novelty crops because it will be a novelty if you get anything at harvest time! These crops are not made for this area. They were made for somewhere else - Yuma, Camp Verde, southern California. Probably for that very reason, people are simply compelled to try to grow them. Love that challenge!

Watermelon & Cantaloupe Melons require heat, warm nights and lots of water. There are some varieties in the catalogs that have been hybridized for colder climates. With a lot of care and extra attention it can be done.

Cucumbers My own miserable experience with cucumbers has me put them in this category. I have tried multiple varieties, I have tried every warm spot in the yard. Most years the plants don't even live long enough to have a flower much less a cuke. Once when I was lamenting the dilemma to a Farm Stand customer and blaming it on living in Cheshire, the woman who lives directly behind me said, "Last year we had so many cucumbers I didn't know what to do with them!" I was surprised she was still standing after the withering glance I threw her way. I know people in Flagstaff's banana belt who grow them and others scattered around town, but there are many like myself who have not had any luck with them.

Try starting them indoors two weeks early. Plant the seedlings in a sunny area and place a hot cap over the plant for the first couple of weeks. My fellow gardener, David, insists on starting his cucumbers directly in the warm soil. That choice may depend on your particular micro-climate.

Give them lots of water once they start to set fruit. As with squash, black plastic may be helpful.

Both bell peppers and jalapenos flourish in Dave Menne's garden as they soak up the heat from walls of water and a block wall.

Peppers Hatch, New Mexico, chili capitol of the world! A visit to Hatch will help you understand the uphill battle we face in growing peppers. In Hatch summer temperatures in the summer are in the 90's with the lows dropping into the 60's. There is abundant water from the Rio Grande, the soil is loose sand.

Everything they have, we don't and therein lies the problem. You can provide water, and amend the soil with organic material and add sand but HEAT is not easy to manufacture. My friend, David, has successfully grown all types

of peppers in Flagstaff and says that the secret is in keeping the plastic 'wall of water' around them for the entire summer. It is important to open the wall to full width once they begin to emerge from it to ensure good air circulation and allow the peppers to be pollinated. Black plastic also helps, and the two can be used together. David has some pepper plants up against a rock wall to keep them warmer at night. Like tomatoes they may benefit from growing in a black pot. Obviously they need to go in the ground as plants, either plants you buy or start inside yourself. Increase pollination with the use of a small paint brush on the blossoms which open mid-morning.

There are so many varieties of peppers I have lost

track of them! From small to large, hot to mild, in every color imaginable. What you grow will depend on what your intended use and what you like to eat. David's favorite varieties are Goliath hybrid, Volcano, Fat n' Sassy, Costa Rican Sweet pepper (red) and the Golden Giant hybrid sweet pepper. David gets most of his pepper (and tomato) seeds from Totally Tomatoes.

Corn Corn will grow here and is great fun especially for children. I think people feel a garden isn't really a garden without corn! The biggest problem with corn is that it takes up a lot of space on small lots. Remember you should not plant corn in a sraight row as it needs to cross pollinate. Corn needs to be planted in a block. As the

tassel matures the pollen drifts down to the corn silk which has emerged from the ear of corn. Each silk pollinated will result in a full kernel on the ear of corn! That is why you sometimes see home-grown corn that is very blotchy with missing kernels, due to poor pollination. To assist the pollination, lightly grasp and strip the pollen from the top of the stalk. Sprinkle the pollen onto the silk emerging from each ear.

Corn also needs a fair amount of water and draws lots of nutrients out of the soil. You can make better use of your space by planting pole beans with the corn, which will climb the stalks. Pumpkins planted nearby will wind their way through the stalks. Master gardener Jim Mast grew corn successfully here for years and recommends Mothers' Day week-end as the time to plant your corn! There are all sorts of new varieties and many suited for northern gardens.

Broccoli and Cauliflower Surprised I am including these? They should do well in a mountain climate as they are cold hardy. They take up a fair amount of space and produce what seems to me a very small amount of produce for the space and effort required. They might be fun to try as an experiment, but if you do plant them carefully consider your use of garden space.

Garden pests do seem to love broccoli and cauliflower. Finding a green worm in your veggies is a bit unappetizing. Even with our diminished insect problems in Flagstaff, if there is an

insect it will devour these so check out some of the organic pest controls. Sometimes, it is easier to just pick the pest off the produce and squish it - so much for Gandhi! Some sources recommend that you not plant broccoli and cauliflower in the same space as previously held by the cabbage family. The seeds are fairly easy to manage and can be sewn directly into warm soil, spacing plants 18-24 inches apart. The stalk emerges from the warm soil and the leaves begin to spread outward with the head in the center. The speading leaves may touch but should not be too crowded. After cutting the central head, side shoots will emerge, extending the harvest if the gardener is diligent in cutting them, rather than allowing the plant to go to seed.

In conclusion, my grandmother would never have grown any of these, too much trouble, time and effort with too little results. But for the modern gardener we have the luxury of experimenting with new plants and seeds because at least for now, we are not dependent on our crops to get us through the cold winter.

~ Vegetables in Containers ~

Almost everything you can grow in the garden you can grow in a container. That is good news if you have a small area! As mentioned, all my tomatoes are grown in black pots. I have two small animal troughs that have holes for drainage. I use these for lettuce, but they would be great for herbs, flowers or beans. Squash, beans, lettuce, chard, peas, herbs, flowers of all kinds can be grown in containers, some even do better in a container!

The exception is perennials. It is not wise to put any perennial in a pot. It is very hard on them over the winter as the pot continually gets warm then very cold. It is also difficult to keep it watered. Three important things about container growing. Make sure the pot is adequate for what you are potting. For vegetables I like a pot to be at least 12 inches deep. Squash need a good sized pot. You need to use really good soil, potting mix, compost. You will probably need to use some sort of fertilizer as the plants confined condition makes it difficult to get the need nutrition. You must water every day! This is essential. The pots dry out so quickly, much faster than plants that are in the ground. Watering everything in pots needs to be part of your daily schedule.

Some Quick Tips On Herbs:

Parsley does extremely well here and is cold hardy. Try it indoors in a pot throughout the winter.

Basil you can't give it too much heat! Do whatever you need to keep it warm, at least 50 degrees at night. Basil won't resent up to 100 degrees during the day. Stick with the common Genoa Basil for best results.

Garlic Chives, on left

Dill easy at 7000 feet, easily re-seeding.
Rosemary If you bring this tender perennial in each fall, it could live for years.
Cilantro you need to plant successively to ensure a steady supply during the growing season. Once cilantro bolts, seemingly overnight, pull it up.
Lavender does well.
Cat Mint known as Cat Nip when dried, is a lovely flowering shrub and provides entertainment for your cat. I have a friend whose cat sits right in the middle of the mint, eyes closed in sheer ecstasy.

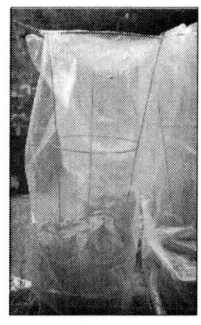

Basil flourishs when left under plastic all summer.

Chapter 9

TOOLS OF THE TRADE

Since gardening is such a popular hobby you can be sure there are those vigorously trying to sell you products and services, most of which you don't need. I have purchased very few tools through retail outlets. Electrical or motorized tools tend to scare me. I enjoy doing everything by hand. For some of you the FUN is in the garden gadgets, automatic sprinkler or drip system, rototiller, chipper shredder, ridding mowers, cold frames, greenhouses and hoop houses to name a few. If this is you, go for it!

Here is my list of simple tools for the garden:

~ Essential Tools ~

Shovel - I prefer the short handled ones, because I am short, easier for me to handle.
Garden fork - Heavy duty with thick tines. A garden fork is a smaller version of a pitch fork.
Leaf Rake - Thin flexible aluminum tines
Yard Rake - Heavy duty steel tines
Trowel or hand shovel. You can't have too many of these. I buy every one I see at garage sales as I like to have several around the yard. I am always misplacing them.
Dandelion Digger
Hand Clipper - Good quality! I have purchased all my good clippers, paying at least thirty dollars a pair. This is the one place not to cut corners, the same goes for flower shears or clippers.

Large Clipper - for small limbs and shrubs
Wheelbarrow - A size you can easily manage. I like the smaller plastic ones as I can barely move the big steel ones even when they are empty.
Five Gallon Buckets
Compost Bin(s) These are usually converted garbage cans with an 80 gallon capacity. I have used plastic garbage cans with the bottom cut out as well.
Gloves I am obsessive about protecting my hands. Dirt under the fingernails is not fun. Working in the yard, my hands are cut, cracked and bleeding in no time. So I take a little extra care to protect my hands.

    1) Try A&D ointment, olive oil or cocoa butter.
    2) Use cotton gloves.
    3) When using latex, vinyl or rubber gloves (for washing
       dishes), I double-layer, pulling the cotton ones
       out to let them dry as my hands get sweaty. For
       safety, don't use heavier work gloves when you will
       be in dirt or water, pulling weeds or trimming.

~ Watering ~

2-3 Watering Cans - Think recycling! Plastic gallon milk jugs with the top sliced off are good for dipping water out of large containers such as collection bins below the gutters. I usually have at least 10-20 of these around the yard.
Plastic Garbage Cans or bins for water collection or storage. I have one under every downspout, and several in the yard and ditch for easy watering.

 CAUTION ! Never leave buckets of water around if you have small children as they can drown in a bucket. Cover the buckets with screen or cloth to protect birds, animals and beneficial insects from falling in and not being able to get out. When my young grandsons come over, I make sure they are all empty.

~ Other Items ~
Child **Paint Brushes** or q-tips for pollinating
Coffee Filters to line pots
Clothes Pins all sorts of uses
Laundry Baskets to cover tender plants during frost. I have found that these are the best protection for young squash plants (T&E). They nest easily and can be brought out only when you need them. For severe cold, cover the basket with a sheet.
Teaspoon or baby spoon to use for seedling transplant.
Bucket of MID-SIZED **Rocks**. These are handy to hold down plastic or support for a plant.
Saucers
Stakes: bamboo, wood or metal stakes of all sizes.

~ Seeds ~
I buy all my seeds from mail order catalogues* where I find a greater variety. After ordering early, the seeds arrive in January, allowing me to start my garden while the snow still covers the ground and temperatures drop below freezing.

Catalogues offer larger quantities of seeds. A small packet of beans in a retail outlet will run between $1.30 - $4.00. Mail order catalogues may sell a half pound of seed for $6.00 - $7.00. This bag of beans will last through several growing seasons. Seeds generally don't go "bad" although the retail stores would like you to think so. Each year their percentage of germination may drop, requiring the gardener to plant a few extra. I once found a whole bag of seed packets in the trash that were fifteen years old. I had no idea where they had been kept or how they had been stored. Eighteen squash seeds germinated in one of the packets. The flowers and other vegetables all had great germination rates as well.

Some gardeners arrange to share an order with another gardener or trade seeds. One person may buy beans while the other will buy peas. When first trying a new vegetable or flower, it is often best to start with a small packet to ensure that you like growing it and that the plant does well. Some items don't warrant a large packet of seed.

~ **Books** ~
I have been very pleased with anything by Eliot Coleman. I have worn thin his book, The New Organic Gardener. Barbara Damrosch's book, The Garden Primer, is a complete guide on almost everything you would need to know on gardening and the resource book I go to first with any questions.

* See pages 97 and 98 for a list of seed catalogues.

Chapter 10

EVERYTHING I NEED FOR THE YARD,
I FOUND IN THE TRASH

You can spend a fortune at the local nursery or home improvement store in paying full price for everything from plants to soil and pots. I prefer the TREASURE HUNT known as bulky trash day. This is the designated day that neighborhoods set out their "too big for the garbage can" items on the curb for the Sanitation department to pick up. At first I limited myself to bags of leaves, always going at night. Then, I moved to early morning, disguising myself with a hat and long coat. Now, I mark the day on the calendar, inspecting the offerings in broad daylight. I freely talk about my treasures with anyone who will listen - just short of bragging about my discoveries!

So, for the record, last year I found:
> 2 bird baths
> 2 compost bins
> 1 wrought iron spiral plant holder
> 1 trellis
> 3 hoses in perfect condition
> numerous large black plastic pots
> terra cotta pots
> numerous mixed size pots
> potting soil within the pots
> bag of un-opened potting soil
> hanging baskets
> live petunia
> wheelbarrow
> air-mattress (to cover compost)
> seeds
> several plant stands
> tomato cages

This is not to mention what I found for myself and for the grandchildren:
Three bikes, a dresser, a doll house, a slide, clothes, dolls and toys, a record player for my niece and a bread machine for my son. Both had requested these items the week before!

I go to the older, middle-income, established neighborhoods for the best results. The more expensive the house, the less likely the chance of finding anything good. I concentrate on my own neighborhood but if I am in another area of town I don't hesitate to scrounge. Legally, once an item is set on the curb, it is open season, fair game! The other great advantage to the great treasure hunt is in keeping recyclable items out of the landfill. I often pick up things with the intention of depositing them in my recycle bin.

~ Garage Sales ~
Here is another great place to pick up garden items, especially garden tools. I buy every trowel I see, usually for as little as 25 cents. I need a lot of them, mostly because I misplace them. I like to have them in a number of places in the yard as trowels are the tool I use the most.

At moving sales, inquire about pots, Miracle Gro fertilizer or other items you are interested in. I find that in asking for the 6 packs or quart-sized pots, people say, "Oh, I have a whole box of those. I didn't think anyone would want them." The same is often true with Miracle Gro or other garden products as I hear, "I do have that. I forgot about those bottles". Many people will give these products away for free or at a low price.

Craigs List is another resource for items useful in the garden. (www.craigslist.com)

~ Ask Around ~
Finally, let people know what items you hope to find. After the Christmas holiday I'll advertize: "Unwanted plants, dead or alive, no questions asked!" I get lots of stuff. Poinsettias are especially good as they come in a nice pot with good potting soil, foil and a bow.

Some plants can be revived, others are gone for good! If I'm concerned with a dead or dying plant about spores in the soil or an insect infestation, I'll leave the pot outside to freeze for a number of nights. This usually guarantees that any pathogens are dead. Since I use this soil to start geraniums, this has never been a problem. We sell the plants at the church garage sale or our annual craft sale with the proceeds going to world-wide missions.

Chapter 11

GARDENING WITH CHILDREN

Expose your children to gardening! Sometimes this works, developing a life-long passion for gardening. Sometimes it doesn't. At age thirty two, the only garden flower my daughter, Lisa, can name correctly is the tulip. My son, Mike, loved gardening right from the start and won numerous awards at the county fair. He can still name almost every plant in any garden. Joey had zero interest. I happened to walk outside in the front yard just in time to hear a frustrated eleven year-old Mike trying to educate his reluctant six year-old brother.

"Joey, what is that flower?"

Mike pointed to a veronica. Joey looked blank. He obviously didn't know the answer. Mike offered a hint.

"It starts with a V."

"Virgin?" asked Joey.

With that Mike got on his bike and rode off. To my knowledge that was the end of Joey's floricultural education. Shawn, my youngest son, loved being IN the garden! His interest was in bugs, snakes and his "pet" spiders or whatever creature he might find under the rocks.

Encourage children by giving them their own small area where they can plant a few of the hardiest plants. I suggest that if they want to try the harder varieties, tell them, "If what you grow this year does well and you take care of it, then you can try that next year."

I recommend daylilies for future flower lovers. They are indestructible, easy and enjoyable for children to grow. I have one large clump of lilies that never bloomed for ten years. They WOULD have bloomed but they were lain in or used for games of hide and seek. Bikes were thrown on top of them. The dogs roamed through them. They survived all the abuse!

Children enjoy planting bulbs. Bulbs are useful to teach delayed gratification! Crocus, grape hyacinths, tulips, glory of the snow and daffodils are all good. I would especially recommend the crocus as they are up so early and the daffodil because they are practically guaranteed to bloom each year. Planting the bulbs in an area on the south side, near the house, is good as the children are able to enjoy watching them emerge as early as January.

With annual flowers, children enjoy cosmos, nasturtiums and sunflowers. Both the nasturiums and sunflowers begin with fairly large seeds, easier for small fingers to manipulate. Children enjoy the heady results of a large sunflower at eye level as they bloom.

As for vegetables, every child should grow pumpkins at least once. What a great variety they have to choose from in considering what will be the biggest or the best! The girls might like the little miniature pumpkins and the boys might like the largest size as they try to grow a giant pumpkin. I really like the old heirloom, New England pie pumpkin, as it's name implies this nice size variety is great for pies. Children with active imaginations will also enjoy the gourds. Remember to soak the seeds on both of pumpkins and gourds for better germination.

Beans are another good 'kid' vegetable. My twin grandsons, at age two, were able to plant several pots by themselves. The seeds are easy for them to handle. The plants grow fast to satisfy their shorter attention spans. They find it fun to grow green, purple and yellow varieties together. Pole beans are fun, when grown over a 'tee-pee' frame of twine, creating a little "fort" for the kids to play in as the vines creep up the poles.

I've often wondered why so many adults want children to grow radishes. Why? The reward for all their time, watering and watching, is something that I consider to taste terrible!

As the plants begin to mature, allowing the children to help water other areas of the garden is always fun. Let them cut some flowers for bouquets. I have been careful to leave the garden chore of weeding till they are older when they are able to distinguish between the weeds and the seedlings. (T&E) Fortunately, I enjoy weeding even if many people do not.

Harvesting is the reward for all of us so be sure to include them in this activity. The time spent, investing in a child, pays off in great rewards. Gardening builds relationships and character. All the beds behind the house were built by my son, Mike. Of course, it wasn't totally due to his love of gardening. He was usually working off being grounded. We still have a great relationship, in and out of the garden

Why try to explain miracles to your kids
when you can just have them plant a garden.
~ *Robert Brault*

Chapter 12

WHAT TO DO WITH ALL THE PRODUCE?

So, you've invested the time in your garden. Plants are growing by inches, produce is hanging from the plants. You're successful! Now what?

Worrying about what you are going to do with excess produce is like wondering what you would do if you had a million dollars! Wait till it happens, then worry about it! There are so many options, believe me, this won't be a problem.

-You can freeze it. Here is a great tip I got from an eighty year-old farmer for freezing squash and many other vegetables. Slice or cube the squash, spread on a cookie sheet the chunks not touching. Place the pans in the freezer. When they are frozen, remove with spatula and put in freezer bags for storage.

~ Dehydrate or dry them.

~ Take vegetables to church. I have sold vegetables at church for years for various missions projects. It is a great treat for all the people who don't have gardens. Set out a small container for the money you will collect from purchases, checking it after each event.

~ Take it to work. Maybe there is an employee who has special needs. People can donate toward helping with that need and get some fresh veggies.

I put a reasonable price on the vegetables and flowers for sale. If you put "donation" only, people are very reluctant to pick things up. They are not sure what "donation" is acceptable and they hesitate. Setting a price is helpful to them. More often than not they put more than the given price in!

Don't want to bother with money - You can also simply give the produce away. Set it out on a table with a free sign. I prefer this over giving people a bag of veggies. People will never refuse a bag of veggies, but they may not like what you are giving them. When you have it set out for free, they take what they want in the amount they want.

~ Trade veggies. I trade veggies for the delicious baked goods from my neighbor, Kay. We're both happy! Another lady happily trades organic eggs for my produce.

~ Donate to a soup kitchen or local shelter.

~ The Neighborhood Farm Stand ~
I've always had a goal to have excess vegetables so I could sell them. First, I set them on a counter at church with a small collection tin, donating the proceeds to mission projects. When I turned fifty years of age I asked myself, "What do I want to do to celebrate my 50th year. What have I never done?"

I wanted to have a Farm Stand! So, that summer, I began preparations for my first Farm Stand. My kids laughed at me through-out the summer. And, as my daughter told me a few years later, "Mom, we're still laughing".

The first year, in August, as the garden began to produce, I set out a white board I had pulled from the trash along with a computer table. I only had some beans and squash along with the pay can. The first day I made two dollars. I was so excited I hung the two dollars on the refrigerator where it remained the rest of the year!

Every year the stand got bigger. My husband made a beautiful garden cart with a roof out of a discarded bicycle baby carrier. I started selling lettuce with edible flowers, I offered chard, kale and cherry tomatoes. People came in droves! One year someone asked me what I had the most of and I truthfully said, "Customers!"

Surprisingly, the favorite item is squash. Everyone wants squash. Many say it is the most beautiful squash they have ever seen.

I love doing the Farm Stand as I have so much fun. I have met so many great people and many new friends. One day three women were chatting away at the Farm Stand when a couple came by. After listening for a few minutes the husband observed, "You all must be good friends."

They looked at each other, started laughing and said, "Well, we know each other from the Farm Stand!"

As the fall season arrives and the garden draws to a close, I usually break down and cry as I begin to put everything away. I've had so much fun and now it is over for the year. But along with all those sports fans, I say, "Wait till next year, bigger and better!

There is a time for everything,
and a season for every activity under the sun . . .

I know that there is nothing better for men
than to be happy and do good while they live.
That everyone may eat and drink
and find satisfaction in all his toil -
this is the gift of God.

Ecclesiastes 3: 1, 12-13

Seed Catalogues

There are an abundance of wonderful catalogues out there! I find it is best to select a few that are good for your own purpose and buy from them. Shipping and handling costs will become unreasonable if you order from too many companies. You may miss out on bulk discounts or special offers if your order is small. I often stagger orders, ordering a lot from a particular catalogue one year, a lot from a different catalogue the next year.

Harris Seeds
Box 24966
Rochester, NY 14624
www.harrisseeds.com

Most of my seeds come from this fine catalogue. They are based in New York state and sell to both professional growers and home gardeners. They have great customer service, and as I mentioned in the sunflower section, their resident farmer, Jeff Werner, is an exceptional resource.

Pinetree Garden Seeds
Box 300
New Glouster, ME 04260
(207) 926-3400

Based in Maine, with conditions similar to Flagstaff, I order frequently from this catalogue. They have a great lettuce mix. They also offer smaller packages of seeds at a very reasonable price. This catalogue is great when trying some new varieties to see how they do in your garden.

Henry Fields
Box 397
Aurora, IN 47001
(513) 354-1494
HenryFields.com

This nursery has a great variety of vegetable and flower seeds offered at good prices. I can buy seeds like beans and squash in bulk and get a very reasonable price. For instance, in 2010 pole beans are 1.95 a packet and 6.95 for a half pound. A one ounce packet of spagetti squash is 4.95. That is going to last for years! I have been pleased with the perennials I have purchased from them at a very reasonable price. Henry Fields and Gurnseys catalogues appear very similar and I believe they share resources.

Totally Tomatoes
334 West Stroud Street
Randolph, WI 53956
(800) 345-5977
www.totallytomatoes.com

I have not ordered from Totally Tomatoes but most of my gardening friends do so. They are very pleased with the seeds they have received. One shared a Bush Golaith start with me and the tomatoes were large and meaty. They seem to be the most complete source for tomatoes and all types of peppers.

Bluestone Perennials
7211 Middle Ridge Road
Madison, OH 44057
(800) 852-5243
www.bluestoneperennials.com

If you are looking for new varieties and new ideas, Bluestone is great! They carry items I haven't seen elsewhere. This is where I got most of my original perenials. Their prices have gone up a lot since I first started ordering from them. This is a good place to share an order with a friend. The success rate with the stock I have received from this is close to 95 percent. You can't beat that!

Both Burpee and Park Seed Nurseries have good reputations among my gardening friends.

Netherland Bulb Company
13 McFadden Road
Easton, PA 18045
www.netherlandbulb.com

For spring-flowering bulbs, including tulips, daffodils and crocus, I have been very happy with Netherland Bulb. If you can hold off till later in the year or after January, you can pick up great sales from them. Most bulb catalogues greatly reduce their prices on remaining stock after the holidays. They also sell in huge quantities for additional savings.

Acknowledgements

To my Grandmother, Mathilda Benson, 1870-1963 whose life has always inspired me.

My Dad, Verner Gustav (Spud) Benson, 1914-1981 humorous writer and cartoonist. A great Dad who encouraged me in every endeavor and taught me to garden.

To ChooChoo McDonald for his excellent craftsmanship on a variety of garden projects.

To my brother in-law, Dennis McDonald, better than a real brother, entertaining, helpful in lots of ways and making me laugh for over 40 years . . . . that could be my next book.

My friend, David Menne, from who I have gleaned numerous valuable garden tips for over 30 years.

My wonderful neighbors for 33 years, Tom and Kay Whitham. Tom, who was raised on a tree farm in Iowa and is a biologist, is like living next to PBS, a Public Broadcasting Station. Kay can do wonders with my veggies in the kitchen. I grow, she cooks, we're both happy.

My four great kids, Lisa, Mike, Joey and Shawn who all helped dragging, carrying, moving, lifting, loading and planting. Making lots of fun of Mom but also very encouraging.

John Winnicki for more truck loads of manure than I can count.

Jim Mast for his helpful seminars, who is very approachable and willing to share his garden expertise. I first met Jim at the Coconino County Fair, a great place to learn about flowers and vegetables.

Ruth - This is a real book! You might have been reading a garden pamphlet, poorly organized, incomplete, no pictures, poor sentence structure, misspelled words and bad grammar.